Towards a Social Grammar of Language

Matthew C. Grayshon

MOUTON · THE HAGUE · PARIS · NEW YORK

ISBN: 90-279-7633-3
Cover design by Jurriaan Schrofer
Printed in the Netherlands

Contents

Introduction

'Two of the fundamental goals of linguistics are
the development of a general theory of human
language behaviour and the development of
appropriate procedures for the full characteriza-
tions of any language' (C.A. Ferguson 1971).

The origin of this work lies in my teaching days in Nigeria between 1950
and 1960. Two questions continually occurred: (1) Why could I not, as a
listener, assess when two people were angry, happy, etc., when I
overheard a conversation in certain Nigerian languages, but could do so
with other languages as, of course, I can do in English? (2) Why was it so
much more difficult for Yoruba students to learn to *speak* English than
for Hausa students? Gradually a third question arose; despite Ferguson's comment above, current linguistic theories as far as I could explore
them up-country in Nigeria were of little help.

On my return to U.K. I continued to work with Overseas teachers at
Nottingham University, many of them speaking tonal languages, and
found that neither linguists in general nor grammarians and phoneti-
cians in particular were asking the questions that I wanted answered.
Gradually two facts forced themselves to my attention: the first to do
with language, the second to do with language operating in society.
First, then, was the function of those features of language usually
termed paralinguistic in the communication process. These included
intonation, stress, pause, timbre, etc. (Crystal 1969).[1] They seemed
quite different in, for example, Yoruba or Nupe and English. To

1. I use Crystal's terminology and from now on will use the symbol I.S. to cover these
features in their many combinations in English. Only when the text necessitates it will I
distinguish between them. However, Crystal follows traditional descriptions of form; I shall
proceed differently.

anticipate, Yoruba uses them more to change the meaning of words, i.e., semantically, whilst English uses them over the whole of a sentence for more social and emotional functions. At the same time I noticed that some students had difficulty in certain social uses of language. A typical example shows itself in student/staff relationships. The course I am mainly involved in has mature, experienced teachers and Training College lecturers as students. We build up close familiar relationships, and mostly we are on Christian name terms; sometimes students from strong hierarchical societies had difficulties, and I occasionally had a progression – Mr. Grayshon sir, Mr. Grayshon, Matthew sir, Matthew – over a period of months. Here we have some form of social constraint over language usage. I have yet to determine which influence is stronger: is it a language form from the mother tongue which is causing interference or is it a social inhibition showing in language?

Also watching language in schools and listening to recordings from a large number of radio programmes I began to formulate some questions:

How is authority shown in language?
How is emotion shown in language?
Just who can say what to whom in what circumstances?
Are the carriers of this social information the same in all languages?

I wondered if it would be possible to formulate a theory to produce answers to my questions. Eventually I began to see that the two sets of questions were related. Gradually the need for a description of language according to function rather than form began to impress itself upon me.

More and more my attention was drawn to I.S. and the difference in function between English and other languages, particularly tonal languages. The normal linguistic descriptions produced books such as Dunstan (1969) and Allen and Van Buren (1971). These give comparison of *forms* of language but no view of function. They also face the investigator with a highly complex analysis (Doke 1954, p. 44). However if we change the question and ask what function I.S. carries with regard to context then we find a different logic and apparently a much simpler description. In some tonal languages (Pike 1946) it changes the meaning of words, i.e., it has a semantic function. In at least one African language it indicates tense change (Nida 1957, p. 128) where the future is indicated by a high tone on the pronoun, the present by a medium tone, the past by a low tone. In some Bantu languages it is used to differentiate the second and third person pronouns (Nida 1957, p. 113). Thus it is used in a grammatical context. In English the use is rather different; it is concerned with emotions and grammatical functions, and these grammatical functions are closely related to social function.

Some of the empirical work which helped to develop my ideas will be found in Chapter 3. These have to do with Nigerian tonal languages and English. This work drew my attention to language as an example of human individual and social behaviour; I argue this in Chapter 1. From this has come the attempt to analyse language as function. It follows that if language is an expression of human behaviour and if we are concerned with language function, one at least of the determiners, and therefore describers, would be social relationships. This might sound as though this is just another example of a sociolinguistic approach. This is not so because sociolinguists take traditional linguistic descriptions and apply them to society or describe society and its complexities by means of the language used. Social grammar is interested in forming a description of language based upon language function in society. This, whilst it will be heavily indebted to normal linguistic descriptions, is closely involved in the relationships of individuals and groups in society.

It is only recently that I have found similarities to my approach in the work of Burling (1970) who says:

> ... I am not concerned with the way in which the rest of culture is dependent upon or similar to language, but I am concerned instead with the way in which language is affected by the rest of culture. On the other hand, unlike most linguists, I am not primarily concerned with the internal structure of language, but only with the way that structure is affected by and dependent upon other things than language. I am convinced that not even the structure of language can be decently understood without some understanding of the animal that uses language and of the setting within which he speaks.

My work is the study of language as social activity, hence the idea of social grammar which will generate the answers to the questions above but will also handle questions such as:
(a) How is English used to show politeness, sincerity, conviction etc.?
(b) Is it possible for an inferior to show anger to and against a superior?
(c) How does an utterance show class, stratification, social relationships?
(d) How do utterances reveal subcultures?
(e) Are the deprivations at the utterance level significant to the individual within his status in society – and in his social role?
(f) When a non-English speaker learns English what elements of social experience cause interference?
This all suggests that we seek our universals for locating in the society in which language itself functions. As I explicate fully in Chapter 2, I initially postulate three. *First* status, which defines who has the power to

determine what language can be used by whom in what situations. An order, for example, requires a superior and inferior and implies power to insist upon it being carried out. An order by an inferior to a superior is classified as insubordination, cheekiness, rudeness, etc. *Secondly* solidarity, the individual relationship where friendship modifies status and allows many more language expressions because of the reduction of the status gap. *Thirdly* emotion which is normally prescribed by status, i.e., who CAN show anger to whom in what circumstances is determined by the status superior; but *in extremis* strong emotion overrules both status and solidarity. All these relationships are expressed in different levels of communication in different language groups.

Social grammar would work in two ways – it would describe these differences but also, by following the description of a language, allow inferences about the nature of the society. But more than this a social grammar might well reveal and describe levels of mother-tongue interference. It ought also to be of use in sociolinguistics, as it would provide a theoretical framework for much current work – a physiological description rather than the present anatomical description presented by systemic grammarians or transformationalists. It has implications for second-language teaching, social anthropology, comparative descriptions of language and the history of language. These are briefly discussed in Chapter 4.

Because of the nature of a book this work is written in consecutive sections, but it is not a linear development. Chapter 1 which is largely epistemological, was conceptually developed after the following sections but could well precede them logically. Chapter 2 discusses the societal determinants of language, whilst Chapter 3 discusses the function of I.S. in English and contrasts this with some other languages. The more empirically minded might prefer to start with either of these two chapters. As I have just mentioned Chapter 4 explores some of the implications of a social grammar for other social sciences.

PRESENTATION

This study is written in the first person. I have deliberately eschewed the laborious, sometimes confusing style of the third person, the passive tense, the royal 'we'. As I discuss more fully in Chapter 1, the suggestion that the use of these devices is 'more academic' and therefore 'more accurate' is a cultural one and is not necessarily so.

It seems to have its origin partly in the idea that a 'mystery' needs to be wrapped up in a special language so that only initiates can really understand, and partly in the convention that there is 'formal' language and 'informal' language and that 'formal' language is in some strange way more 'accurate', more 'objective', 'better'. (This is discussed in some of its aspects in Strang [1970, esp. pp. 79 and 105]). Both these ideas are no longer tenable. It is most unacademic to wrap up findings so that the communication process hinders the message rather than assists it, and recent work in the sociology of knowledge has thrown into question the whole concept of 'objective' knowledge (*Cf.* Berger and Luckman 1966, Kuhn 1970). More interesting, for this study, is the evidence by Labov (Williams 1970, pp. 167–169) in which he analyses the language of a middleclass speaker in the U.S.A. and shows that its apparent verbal expertise and superiority over Negro dialect can be mostly appearance and that in fact a whole conversation comes down to two statements which are mutually contradictory. Allied to this is the choice of vocabulary. To anticipate Section 2, Part 2, so often those elements of our vocabulary associated with the high status elements of society are used/utilised because they show/indicate that accuracy lies in/within the sole prerogative of the power/intellectually superior section of society. As Chief Inspector Eric Cheetham said in Blackpool's magistrate's court:

I understand Tamadonn is shortly marrying an English girl and, therefore, there will be reticence on the part of the Home Office in escalating his departure (*The Guardian* newspaper Nov. 1970).

In this work I am dealing with utterances, the sounds in all their order and range, at work in society.

Over the centuries spoken English has changed and adapted in so many ways. Regrettably the written word has been left behind and has become a different creature. As Strang (1970, p. 161) points out this starts as early as the period 1370 to 1570. Already by 1711 word play is made with written ambiguities; this might read well in *The Spectator* (Strang 1970, p. 142), but if a worker in language is unaware, or only partially aware, he finds himself in the situation I comment upon when discussing transformational grammar. Reading now requires almost an act of translation, certainly a complex act of interpretation, of relating words on paper to the complex audio/aural/visual procedure of non-written communication - for example, the convention of spelling so that overseas students can worry about the difference between 'I shall' and 'I will' when we actually say 'I'll' in both cases. The problem caused by the visual requirement of reading from paper of having a space between words. In Nottingham there is a phoneme cluster /'mekiga'bækadz / which appears in writing as 'make it go backwards' and which is interpreted, when referring to a car, as 'put it in reverse'; /'mekiga'bæ-kadz / is, in speech, all one utterance, heard as such and comprehended as such. The problem is not confined to the teacher and child who have to make a relationship between the visual 'He put it in reverse' and the aural /'mekiga'bækadz /, but as I said above it is a strict awareness of the difference between what we visually represent and what we say, and the gradations between them, that can confuse and limit language research.

I must, therefore, have the courage of my convictions and carry out the advice I have given to class after class of students – to be clear, concise and to stay as close to the spoken word as possible.

A final plea: this study has come out of my daily work and thought and been written up in the 'spare' moments of a normal busy working life and is not as systematic or as polished as I would have liked it to have been if I could have had long periods in which to reflect, write and rewrite. I am only too conscious of its weaknesses and limitations – an educationalist walking through the tangle of the jungle of language description. However what has been said is important; at least I believe so and so do the many students who have encouraged me to write it up. The more discussion, the more criticism and feedback I get then the better the chance of a social grammar of language being produced. It is obvious that I am not 'operating the machine', i.e., working inside an accepted theory. In attempting to propound a new theory I, like Popper, believe in trying to state it as unambiguously as possible so that it can be exposed to comment, and possible refutation. Only by comment, feedback and careful evaluation can knowledge go forward.

Finally my thanks. Thanks above all to numerous students, English, Nigerian and others, who have patiently listened, criticised, suggested, tried out ideas, but above all encouraged. Thanks to Dr. W. Nash, a friend and colleague without whose support and comment this work would never have been completed. As always one is deep in debt to librarians, so thanks to Miss C. Land and her colleagues of the Education Library, Nottingham University. Thanks to typists, principally the late Miss Hickling who toiled for years over my manuscripts. Lastly thanks to all those academics who told me that my work was irrelevant as it did not fit into linguistics, or sociology, or psychology . . . you got me good and mad and I had to finish.

2. See Magee (1973) for an introduction and brief bibliography of Karl Popper's work.

CHAPTER I

Language in Society

A grasp of accomplished natural language cannot be won by focussing on either language or context. Each is barren, and both take on substance when we inquire into the interactive phenomenon of understanding where they flow together into the on-going accomplishment of social realities (R. Kjolseth 1972).

A great deal of work has been done, both empirical and theoretical, in the study of language as a social phenomenon. The whole field of sociolinguistics has grown and been clarified. There is a discussion by Pride (1970) up to 1967, a rather different approach by Robinson (1972) up to 1972; the works edited by Fishman (1968, 1971, 1972; Cf. Fishman et al. 1968), Williams (1970), Whitely (1971), Gumperz (1971), Gumperz and Hymes (1972), Hymes (1964) give an introduction. But the corpus includes work by Bernstein (1972), Lawton (1968) in the field of social class; work in language in education (Open University 1972).[3] However they all have one overriding limitation, to quote Kjolseth (1972, p. 73) again:

... you will also be able to see there the non-isolated, unseparated constitutive act of situated natural language in use – now not as a copy or representation of social action or an external reality, but AS social action and reality.

They deal with social action, group man, group social interactions. I am also concerned with the individual in his relations to the group and to other individuals. It will become obvious that this work is deeply

3. It will be obvious from my bibliography and in the text which writers have been of use.

indebted to insights and evidence from not only sociolinguistics but also anthropology and sociology. Language is not only the product of society and man in society but of man *vis-à-vis* other individuals.

Despite the different approach of sociolinguists, psycholinguists, linguists and myself, we are in search of universals, of 'laws', which will enable us to explain, arrange and sensibly discuss language. However I think that it is important to remember that in the case of language we might well be involved in an impossible job, not so much because of the complexity of the material, though that is certainly a possibility, but because of the nature of man. Pelto (1965) says:

> In fact, the rules of any language can be looked upon as simply a particular clear instance of the generalization that human social behaviour in every society follows regular rules – customs, mores, standards for different situations – that are learned by individuals as they grow up in their particular societies.

But man is also contradictory; he can have blatant contradictions in his own society; he can hold contradictory ideas at the same time; he relies on 'common sense' which is full of contradictions, and these contradictions will show in language in a whole variety of ways. I have yet to find this problem explored and can only point it out as a possible limiting factor in our search. If there is no such thing as an absolutely logical man in an absolutely logical society (even allowing for a whole variety of logics) then how can we hope for absolutely logical descriptions?

Man operates in a society, in a social system in which individuals and groups play various parts or roles in the drama of living, and all the different customs and behaviours in a culture are functionally related. This culture is a way of life; it largely shapes how a man feels, behaves and perceives as he adapts (or does not adapt) to this world. In large communities (for example, England) there are subcultures which have patterns in common with the main culture but which have local variations which set them apart as different. These subcultures may be determined geographically, historically, by class, by job; they may be vertical divisions, horizontal divisions or 'cells' made up of a permutation of others. Class, for example, tends to be a horizontal division showing up all over the country; a regional division, for example Welsh nationalism, is vertical, covering a specific geographical area but encompassing all social classes in that area. 'Cells' can be institutionalised like the police or the army (with classification horizontally in class-officers, N.C.O.s and men; vertically in its county regiments and thus giving 'cells' where there is a sergeants' mess of X regiment which has both commonality and difference with the sergeants' mess of Y regiment) or combination of class, job and geography, e.g., coalminers, Welsh coalminers, Yorkshire coalminers.

By the use of language these groups in society can at the same time relate to each other and yet be separate; can attempt dominance or submission; can argue, fight, or be friendly; can be fully sympathetic or in mutual incomprehension. The individual can either move with his group or against it; he can switch his role and his codes to fit into more than one group. It is these complex social and individual relationships which form the context for my purposes.

The word 'language' is imprecise, as imprecise as the word 'love'. Sometimes the context will give some limitation of definition that is not enough. In this study I am concerned with the spoken language rather than the written so that whenever language is used it means spoken as opposed to written. But it includes those elements referred to as 'paralinguistics' (Crystal 1969) because part of my argument is that certain social information – carried in these features in English – moves to grammatical levels in other languages. Language is also associated with gestures, and communication often utilizes gesture and posture (see, e.g., Birdwhistell 1970, Lamb 1965, Scheflen 1972). Certain African languages utilize posture where English uses semantic and grammatical features (Grayshon 1973). However unless specific mention is made in the text, these kinesic features are not included. The various meanings of the word 'linguistics' can cause confusion; for the purposes of this study I take it in the sense of the study of language in the traditional way, that of the University Department. It has wider and narrower connotations, but these will be made clear at the time of use.

A further problem of definition is in the terms such as sociolinguistics, psycholinguistics, anthropological linguistics. There is danger that there might be an element of the Count Smorltork approach (the Dickens' character who proposed to write an essay on Chinese metaphysics by consulting the encyclopaedia, first on China, then on metaphysics and by combining the resultant information). Is a sociolinguist a sociologist who takes the findings of linguistics and applies them to sociology – or the reverse, a linguist who takes the insights of sociology and applies them to linguistics? Or is there an attempt to develop new insights by other combinations? I would hope that we can develop an approach whereby a variety of insights are utilized as tools to give new insights as to the nature of language and its relationship to society. As this study goes on I shall show the limitations of relying on areas of reified knowledge for explaining language. Before this is done I want to consider further the nature of the social world which is the context and *raison d'être* for language.

SOCIAL REALITY[4]

Berger and Luckman (1966, p. 53) suggest that language is the most important sign system of human society and that 'the common objectifications of everyday life are maintained primarily by linguistic signification'. That 'language originates in and has its primary reference to everyday life; it refers above all to the reality I experienced in wide-awake consciousness, which is dominated by the pragmatic motive (that is, the cluster of meanings directly pertaining to present and future actions) and which I share with others . . .'. Language as a sign system has a facticity external to myself, and it forces a speaker into its patterns inasmuch as the rules of German syntax cannot be used to speak English. 'Language provides me with a ready-made possibility for the ongoing objectification of my unfolding experience' (1966, p. 53). However they go on to point out that language can transcend the 'here and now' and 'bridges different zones within the reality of everyday life and integrates them into a meaningful whole' (1966, p. 54). Language can go on to transcend the reality of everyday life and become symbolic language. On this level language moves into areas that are unavailable to everyday experience: 'Language now constructs immense edifices of symbolic representation that appear to tower over the reality of everyday life like gigantic presences from another world' (1966, p. 55). But language can also bring back these symbols – ' . . . and appresenting them as objectively real elements in everyday life . . . I live in a world of signs AND symbols everyday' (1966, p. 55).

They point out that the social order is a human product ' . . . more precisely, an ongoing human production' (1966, pp. 69–70). So, I argue that as social order is a product of ongoing human activity so is language. Berger and Luckman make the following statement (1966, p. 70); I suggest that for the study of language the word 'language' can be substituted for 'social order':

Social order is not part of 'the nature of things', and it cannot be derived from the 'laws of nature'. Social order exists ONLY as a product of human activity. No other ontological status may be ascribed to it without hopelessly obfuscating its empirical manifestations. Both in its genesis (social order is the result of past human activity) and its existence in any instant of time (social order exists only and in so far as human activity continues to produce it) it is a human product.

4. This section relies heavily on the work of Berger and Luckman (1966).

They go on to discuss habitualization and the origins of institutionalization. It is obvious that language is one of the human activities that
becomes habitualized and institutionalized. For example we can substitute language as a particular habitualized action in this quotation:

> Habitualized actions, of course, retain their meaningful character for
> the individual although the meanings involved become embedded as
> routines in his general stock of knowledge, taken for granted by him
> and at hand for his projects into the future (1966, p. 71).

And again, substituting for 'conduct' in this quote:

> Institutions also, by the very fact of their existence control human
> conduct by setting predefined patterns of conduct which channel it in
> one direction against the many other directions that would theoreti-
> cally be possible. It is important to stress that this controlling
> character is inherent in institutionalization as such, prior to or apart
> from any mechanisms of sanctions specifically set up to support an
> institution (1966, p. 72).

I shall come back again to the primary and secondary social controls
functioning over language and in language.

In the whole of the discussion of this section they argue that through
the growth of habitualization there is institutionalization of behaviour
and that institutions confront an individual as undeniable facts. However the objectivity of the institutional world is a humanly produced and
constructed reality. They make the very important point that '. . . the
relationship between man, the producer, and the social world his
product, is and remains a dialectical one. That is, man (not, of course, in
isolation but in his collectives) and his social world interact with each
other. The product acts back upon the producer. Externalization and
objectivation are moments of continuing dialectical process' (1966, p.
78). They suggest a third moment in the process which is internalization.
They sum this up in the following form:

> Society is a human product. Society is an objective reality. Man is a
> social product (1966, p. 79).

The whole thrust of their argument is to show that the human is
meaningless without the society he has created and that though this
society has objective reality, this very reality is dependent upon the
individual in his social efforts. From this I argue that we must consider
language as objective reality but also as a social product and that
therefore the search for universals must lie in the social world that man
has created. Universals created from an 'objective' study of language as

being 'out there' suffer from weaknesses due to the reification of knowledge; I come back to this later.

In the third section of their book, amongst other things Berger and Luckman (1966, pp. 149–150) discuss the internalization of reality. This will be discussed more fully when we look at the development of language in the individual. The point I wish to make here is that internalization in a general sense is the basis for understanding one's fellowmen and apprehending the world as a meaningful and social reality. So that when Berger and Luckman say:

> This apprehension does not result from autonomous creations of meaning by isolated individuals, but begins with the individual 'taking over' the world in which others already live (1966, p. 150),

I can refer to the special case of the 'world of language' instead of the total 'world'; language is subsumed in the world. Similarly in the next two statements, I could insert 'language' between 'subjective' and 'processes' in the first; and 'language' between 'shared' and 'situation' in the second, and bring out the function and nature of the particular instance of language from the set of total social experience:

> In any case, in the complex form of internalization, I not only 'understand' the other's momentary subjective processes, I 'understand' the world in which he lives, and that world becomes my own. We now not only understand each other's definitions of shared situations, we define them reciprocally. A nexus of motivations is established between us. We are not only living in the same world, we participate in each other's being (1966, p. 150).

One final point, for the time being, from Berger and Luckman. They point out that the most important vehicle for reality-maintenance is conversation, and principally conversation between an individual and the significant others. They make the point that conversation means that people speak with each other but firstly only refer to ' . . . the rich aura of non-verbal communication that surrounds speech', and secondly '. . . that the greater part of reality-maintenance in conversation is implicit, not explicit. Most conversation does not in so many words define the nature of the world. Rather, it takes place against the background of a world that is silently taken for granted' (1966, p. 172).

It is with the analysis of this 'aura of non-verbal' communication that I am concerned because its function in English has sometimes to do with emotion, status and solidarity and therefore reflects social attitudes. If we are to have international social understanding then we must have some way of making explicit the implicit and ordering it in a meaningful cross-cultural way. This is one of the functions of social grammar; later in this work I suggest some approaches to this problem.

In following Berger and Luckman's analysis of social reality I put language firmly as a social process that has grown up in society by the work of individuals operating in a whole variety of social groupings. Just as society can have an objective reality so can language, but this objective reality is always rooted in society and interacts with it. The explanation of society as a dialectical process applies *mutatis mutandis* to language as being part of the set, social reality. This affects where we look for universals to define language; given this analysis we can only find universals in relationships. Further that these relationships are between sections of society and between man and society and between man and man.

SOCIAL TRANSACTIONS

Barth (1966) in his influential paper 'Models of social organization' points out that simple analysis of social forms is not sufficient for social anthropological analysis and that what are needed are generative models. The models he discusses in the paper ' . . . are not designed to be homologous with observed social regularities; instead they are designed so that they, by specific operations, can generate such regularities or forms. They should be constituted of a limited number of clearly abstracted parts, the magnitude or constellation of which can be varied, so that one model can be made to produce a number of different forms' (1966, p. v)

Social anthropology is only of interest in as much as it deals with society in a particular way. Barth quoting Radcliffe Brown suggests that it is the comparative theoretical study of forms of social life amongst primitive people. Language is a form of social life, and therefore we ought to be able to gain insights about language from their work. The main interest in this work will come later when I utilize his description of winter herring fisheries. Now I want to stress the fact that Barth is interested in relationships and action and change, not in static description.

Explanation is not achieved by a description of the patterns of regularity, no matter how meticulous and adequate, nor by replacing this description by other abstractions congruent with it, but by exhibiting what MAKES the pattern, i.e. certain processes. To study social forms, it is certainly necessary but hardly sufficient to be able to describe them. To give an explanation of social forms, it is sufficient to describe the processes that generate forms.

In the following I wish to explore the extent to which patterns of social form can be explained if we assume that they are the cumulative result of a number of separate choices and decisions made by people acting *vis-à-vis* one another. In other words, that patterns are generated through processes of interaction and in their form reflect the constraints and incentives under which people act (1966, p. 2).

Now as language is social act and as so often our choice of language is determined by our social status, and as our language world has been determined by the social processes and relationships through which we have grown up, then we can approach our study of language utilizing the idea of language as a social process. Also utterances are generated by social interaction; by looking at the social relationships and finding the processes that generate the forms we have a tool for describing language. I return to this later. But it is interesting to see how many social judgments Barth makes utilizing language. He describes (pp. 6-10) the situation in the winter herring industry in Norway. He discusses status and the interaction between the skipper, the netboss and the fishermen. Part of his analysis includes comments on utterances made. He points out that the skipper, in this particular situation, cannot maintain the maritime tradition of having the bridge to himself. Barth says (about the fishermen):

... they converse quietly with each other, and savour ...

In the full passage the words 'converse quietly' suggest to the English reader a sense of respect of the men for the skipper. To have made noisy conversation implies disrespect – but this is not necessarily true for all societies.

As for the skipper he, Barth, makes judgments about his behaviour suggesting confidence, knowledge and experience. The implication is that he does so by certain language patterns:

... [he] communicates little, in contrast to the others on the bridge and never elicits comments, evaluations or advice from any other person (1966, p. 8).

Again, about the netboss:

... he is spontaneous, argues and jokes, and gives off evidence of inspired guesswork, flair and subtle sensing. ... he can brag about gambling and drinking bouts ... At the same time his joking behaviour is a constant denial of any claim to authority on the bridge in challenge to the skipper ...

I am interested in how these judgments are made. Why do certain words, constructions and *ways* of saying (i.e., I.S. patterns) reveal authority or shared authority. We read that the netboss by 'joking behaviour' shows that he is not challenging the skipper; however, when the netboss takes charge in the boat Barth says in the continuation of the passage above:

> ... and is in this respect in marked contrast to the institutionalized pattern of gross and continual cursing and assertion of authority on his part during the net casting operation (1966, p. 8).

I find the description 'institutionalized' most interesting as applied to bad language (which phrase is in itself a cultural and not a grammatical description!). Part of assertion of authority lies in a particular type of cursing, i.e., a language pattern. In similar types of authority relationships in other cultures what, if any, language patterns are used to:

(a) deny authority conflict,
(b) assert authority?

For the moment I only wish to point out that indirectly Barth shows to the observer just how much the language patterns have revealed to him, including changes in relationship. I will discuss this later in terms of status and solidarity. It is pertinent to remember that we have seen two ways of utilizing language to assert authority:
1. The skipper by limited language, quietness of utterance and never requiring answers.
2. The netboss by changing from joking, arguing and extravert language behaviour to cursing and absolute command giving.
A social grammar has to be concerned with the social situation which developed these situations, to give some indication to a foreigner how to interpret what is going on and to give rules which allow similar situations to be identified and categorized.

It would seem that Barth's generative model will not only be useful to social anthropologists but also of value in discussing the function of language as a social activity.

GRAMMAR AND THE REIFICATION OF KNOWLEDGE

In the introduction I suggested that I found traditional linguistics of little value in helping me answer questions that had arisen in my experience. It is necessary to examine the reasons for this a little more closely. There are, I suggest, two main reasons – one lies in the very nature of scientific research and the other lies in my approach to language from the social science perspective with a consequential contradiction with the reification of knowledge in the linguistic world outlook.

The argument for my first point is found in Kuhn's 'The structure of the scientific revolution' (1970). He points out that:

Observation and experience can and must drastically restrict the range of admissible scientific belief, else there would be no science. But they cannot alone determine a particular body of such belief. An apparently arbitrary element compounded of personal and historical accident, is always a formative ingredient of the beliefs espoused by a given scientific community at a given time (1970, p. 5).

He goes on to argue (in sections III, IV and V of the book) that

... research (is) a strenuous and devoted attempt to force nature into the conceptual boxes supplied by professional education (1970, p. 5).

This is another way of describing the objectifying of knowledge in Berger and Luckman terms. However Kuhn goes on to argue that science

... is a highly cumulative enterprise, eminently successful in its aim, the steady extension of the scope and precision of scientific knowledge. Yet one standard product of the scientific enterprise is missing. Normal science does not aim at novelties of fact or theory and, when successful, finds none (1970, p. 52).

In this and subsequent pages (e.g., p. 5), he elaborates the point made in the introduction that science deliberately ignores novelty, but that the very nature of research ensures that novelty is not ignored. (This is the dialectic of Berger and Luckman):

... then research under a paradigm changes. That is what fundamental novelties of fact and theory do. Produced inadvertently by a game played under one set of rules, their assimilation requires the elaboration of another set. After they have become part of science, the enterprise, at least of those specialists in whose particular field the novelties lie, is never quite the same again (Kuhn 1970, p. 52).

Am I being too immodest when I suggest that I am in the process of elaborating a new set of rules for a new 'game' in the way we look at language? In Kuhn's terms I am aware of anomaly – that nature has somehow violated the paradigm-induced expectations of current theory; the anomaly must be further explored and the paradigm has to be adjusted. (Or even a new paradigm developed [Kuhn 1970, pp. 52–53]).

At this stage of my thinking it is to suggest that there is a crisis situation (Kuhn 1970, pp 66 ff.) and that out of it there will be new theory that will then dominate research. Though it may be that there will be a new theory that will require comparison with a preceding theory and with nature and thus require validation (Kuhn 1970, pp. 77 ff.), at the moment the most I would claim is that there are anomalies in present theory and that I have suggestions which are drawn from nature. In Berger and Luckman terms I have subjectified my experience of the world, and I am now attempting to objectify it so that it can become a paradigm expounding anomalies in current thought. My suggestion is that current linguistic thought is a product of its own training situation which has laid a deep hold on its practitioner's mind and thus requires him to ignore anomalies for the success of the enterprise. 'Normal science, for example, often suppresses fundamental novelties because they are necessarily subversive of its basic commitments' (Kuhn 1970, p. 5). This is not to suggest that this is immoral or improper behaviour; on the contrary, it is correct; it is part of the evolution of thought. To sum up, then, on this first point: linguists have, of necessity, ignored (or just not seen) certain phenomena. I suggest there is an increasing number of phenomena that don't fit into their scheme, and I am suggesting a way of coping with them.

The second point is that of the reification of knowledge. Berger and Luckman define the reification of knowledge as:

... that reification is the apprehension of human phenomena as if they were things, that is, in non-human or possibly superhuman terms. Another way of saying this is that reification is the apprehension of the products of human activity *as if* they were something other than human products ... Reification implies that man is capable of forgetting his own authorship of the human world ... the reified world is, by definition, a dehumanized world (1966, p. 106).

They go on to point out that the possibility of reification is always very likely as man establishes an objective social world. 'The objectivity of the social world means that it confronts man as something outside himself. The decisive question is whether he still retains the awareness that, however objectivated, the social world was made by men – and therefore, can be remade by them' (Berger and Luckman 1966, p. 106).

GRAMMATICAL FIT

This dehumanized world is seen in the field of linguistics if we think about the old outdated prescriptive grammar. Here were laws not made by man but which determine correctness and are imperatives. The regrettable traces of these can still be seen in the letter columns of our national and local press and are even more common in schools. No serious linguist accepts these grammars, however implicit reification creeps in. Let us look at the concept of grammatical fit. Here we have a form of reification where, I suggest, the terms used in a descriptive grammar have lost their meaning. The case I instance is drawn from a report of a research project by Professor John Sinclair funded by the Social Science Research Council (Sinclair et al. 1971). In it occurs the following passage:

One of the fascinating aspects of this work is the lack of fit between grammatical form and discourse function. For example, one often uses an imperative structure. 'Open the window', to command someone to do something, but one can just as easily, and sometimes more successfully, use an interrogative or declarative:

Would you mind opening the window.
Could you open the window.
That window is still closed.
It's very stuffy in here.

We find that 'softened' commands occur very frequently inside the classroom. The teacher conceals his authority by using a grammatical form which implies that the children have a choice:

Could you all turn to page 17.
Kevin, would you like to do some maths now.

We notice that teachers tend to fall back on imperatives when the children don't do what they are told:

T: Kevin, would you like to do some maths now?
P: NO RESPONSE

T: It's time to do your maths now, Kevin.
P: NO RESPONSE

T: Come and do your maths, Kevin.

Pupils very rarely make mistakes in the interpretation of an utterance and respond to an interrogative command as if it were a question. How do they manage? They need to use two pieces of information about the situation: first, what activities and actions are permissible at a given time – writing, drawing, talking, laughing, eating, are all activities which are allowed at certain times and forbidden at others;

second, what actions are feasible at a given time. Using such information, we can state two rules governing the interpretation of utterances:

1. Any declarative or interrogative clause which is concerned with a forbidden activity being performed by someone inside the classroom is to be interpreted as a command to stop.

Someone is talking	command
Are you eating	command
Is the little boy eating?	question

2. Any interrogative clause with *you* as subject, containing one of the modal verbs, *can, could, will, would,* and describing a feasible action is to be interpreted as a command.

Can you open your books at page 17.	command
Can you swim a length of the baths?	question

We predict that if the last example was uttered at the swimming pool it would be followed by a splash.

Now in this passage there is recognition that there is a difference between grammatical fit and discourse function but there is implicit the idea that grammatical terms such as 'question', 'interrogative' or 'declarative' have a permanency otherwise than that suggested by use and by man's definition.

There is no recognition in a change of function due to changes in society.[5] When we look at the following passage from the point of view of man in society we see that:

The first thing to note is that a command can ONLY be given by a superior. As the English language developed only the superior COULD give an order. Without going into social history it can be said that a superior may well only have bothered to give orders in a form of words and an intonation and stress pattern reserved for inferiors. This can still be seen in institutionalized language such as in the Army, where not only can the inferior not give an order he cannot even question or speak without permission to a superior:

'Permission to speak, Sir.'   'Not granted.'

And that is the end of that.

With his social equals the speaker has to have a different pattern which reflects their relative social status; the nearer equal, the less

5. The original of the discussion that follows was published in an article by Grayshon (1975a).

authoritative can be the form or the intonation and stress. A complex situation might well require complex language usage in this order situation. (For a novelist's handling of this problem see the Hornblower books by C.S. Forester, particularly Hornblower's relationship with Bush, his second-in-command.) The grammatical forms have been determined by the social situation. The grammatical form which is known as a command grew up when superiors ordered an inferior what to do. The request form grew in a condition of social equality. In the example above with Kevin, we have a perfectly good *social* fit, a very good example of social grammar. The social situation as conceived by the teacher suggests that politeness, the language of equals, will lead to a better general social classroom attitude. However as the inferior does not respond so the teacher utilizes increasingly authoritative utterances. There is in social grammar no lack of fit. The superior works his way through a series of utterances, all commands, but varying in 'politeness' and 'authoritativeness'. Both the recipient and the observer recognize a gradation of insistence of obedience; actual action showing obedience comes, varies according to circumstances. Some of these can be determined from the general status situation in a particular sub-culture (it is a very strict school; it is an easy-going school; it is an easy-going school but the staff stand no nonsense) which can be eventually defined in social grammar terms, others depend upon personal interpretations of other individuals – and this is a complex situation to explore and define.

What has happened to the language is that the grammatical forms grew up, so to speak, in very definite social situations which gave them precise patterns. Society changed and instead of changing the patterns, used a sort of 'conservation of matter law', utilized the old forms, gave them a different usage and that was that. So as society has changed, language usage has changed, but the old forms have not, therefore it would seem sensible now to utilize inverted commas for descriptive linguistic grammar terms such as 'interrogative', 'declarative', 'refusal', 'negative', etc., as these terms are not necessarily relevant to language usage and could be replaced by symbols and use the terms more accurately in social grammar usage.

In the example quoted we do not need to say that there is a lack of fit, but that in a status situation modified by a solidarity relationship, the superior had to work through an increasing order of authority utterances to eventually have his command obeyed. It would then be necessary to categorize the utterances used and the features of communication (using perhaps standard linguistic terms) and then move to another language and see how a similar situation developed.

In the development of a social grammar of language we would then go on to categorize the utterance used and the features of communication (using standard linguistic terms) and then move to another language and see how a similar situation developed.

I am indebted to Professor D. L. Bolinger (Grayshon 1975a) for the fruitful suggestion that what happens to a grammatical structure is similar to what has happened to the change in meaning in words. For example, 'I want something to eat' originally was a declaration of lack of food with perhaps a hint that the listener might do something to fulfil the want. Now the 'want' means 'desire' and the 'hint' is now much stronger. In the change of meaning there is the retention of a pivotal meaning which is qualified in use by a particular situation. Very often, both in grammatical structure and in word meaning change, there is a gradual transformation of function *but* the rules of change are to be found not in the forms of the structure but in the social context. In both the case of the teacher giving the order in the various forms, and a series:

'I want something to eat' said the hunter to his rifle.
'I want something to eat' said by one friend to another looking at plates of different sandwiches.
'I want something to eat' said by the husband to the wife.
'I want something to eat' said by the spoilt child to a doting mother.

The key to the differences will be found outside an analysis of forms.

Yet again in the area of tenses we can see a change of meaning not accompanied by 'correction' in grammatical terms.[6] Of course the very nomenclature of tenses is a social one derived from temporal needs, 'present', 'future', 'past'; or manners, 'past conditional', etc. Workers in anthropology have shown that tenses in language are intimately related to the needs and time concepts of the particular language group, and Whorf's hypothesis was initially triggered off because of the different tense construction of the Indian tribe he was studying. However, tense function has changed and the grammatical descriptive terms have not. The most striking example that I know is the present continuous of the verb to have – am having; this in contemporary usage in English has a forward looking implication together with that of promise:

I am having a bicycle at Christmas.

More logically in Nigeria, 'I am having' has more of the original time

6. I am indebted to Dr. Nash of Nottingham University for this example.

content of something happening now, but they use it instead of the present simple 'I have'. Again the past perfect tense of the verb 'to go' used to mean, as its nomenclature implies, some action completed:

I have been to London

meant that I have been and come back and that it is all over and done with. In today's usage it has another meaning, that of the immediate past; indeed on the return journey you are asked by a friend 'Where have you been?' and you reply 'I've been to London' even though you are on the return journey. There is no need to explore this further.

What do we say here, that there is lack of grammatical fit in tense agreement? Possibly, but I suggest we turn it round and see this as an example of society utilizing language at hand to indicate new conditions of living (certainly the Nigerian example has grown up from usage, even though it may indicate a possible example of mother tongue interference) and thus try and categorize it from social relationships. Once again the key to form leads outside the forms themselves.

There are other areas where there is a degree of reification. For example, we have various linguistic categories – jargon, cant, dialect, formal speech, argot, informal speech, manner of discourse, colloquialism. These can be arranged in two groups, the first of which is:

Manner of discourse: 'Variety of language used in a particular situation. Features of pronunciation, grammar and/or vocabulary may indicate a speaker's attitude to the subject under discussion or his social relationship to the intended listener'. Then is listed Joos' 'levels of speech' – (a) frozen or oratorical, formal or deliberate, consultative, casual, intimate; (b) cultivated or cultural (educated speaker of the standard language); (c) colloquial (type of speech used in everyday informal talk); (d) substandard (non-standard, illiterate, vulgar – a type of speech noticeably different from the 'accepted' standard) (Joos 1967).

Then there is a second group:

Jargon: (1) The collective term for the words, expressions, technical terms, etc., which are intelligible to the members of a specific group, social circle or profession but not to the general public (Pei and Gaynor 1954).
(2) A set of terms, expressions used by a social or occupational group but not used and often not understood by the speech community as a whole. Outsiders often regard the jargons such as 'officialese', 'journalese', 'medicalese', etc., as 'bad style'. The sum total of terms used in a particular subject, e.g., chemistry (Hartmann and Stork 1973).

Cant: (1) The special vocabulary of a particular group, especially criminals (Pei and Gaynor 1954).
(2) A jargon peculiar to a local, social or occupational group, particularly of the lower social strata. Alternative terms: argot, lingo (Hartmann and Stork 1973).
Dialect: (1) A specific form of a given language, spoken in a certain locality or geographical area (Pei and Gaynor 1954).
(2) A regional, temporal or social, variety of language differing in pronunciation, grammar and vocabulary from the standard language, which is in itself a socially favoured dialect (Hartmann and Stork 1973).

There are two points to which I want to draw attention: first the degree of tautology in these descriptions – there is a tendency to define against the standard of 'formal' language, which in the case of Pei and Gaynor is defined geographically, and Hartmann and Stork almost meaninglessly in the description under that head, but as a standard in 'colloquialism'; cf. also 'cultivated or cultural' and 'colloquial' under 'manner of discourse'; secondly that all the descriptions are social and/or cultural and in no sense whatever linguistic! There is no attempt at definition according to linguistic forms; there are attempts to show that certain types of language defined socially have certain features, but in the historical and temporal continuum the social definition preceded the linguistic which became an attempt to define and even justify the social categories. These categories will be discussed in a different way later; I only want to make the point here of the importance of the 'formal' or 'standard' which is the language (or dialect) of the status holders. Consequently there is always the suggestion that the formal is an eternal standard out there, a law given rather than a state imposed. One piece of evidence is the idea of the special case of 'formal' in academic circles, where there is considered to be a single way of presenting a thesis and that this way of itself bestows impartiality and superiority. The criterion is not so much

'Is the meaning clear?', but
'Is it in a proper form?'

which implies the reification of the form. It is not created by man and capable of change and modification, but is there with that other partial reification 'academic standards'. This at least partial reification of the idea of standard language, shows in the work done in the American Language Enrichment programmes, where the original concept was of lifting the poor and the deprived (sic) up to a standard. Implicit in much of the work there was the idea of this standard having a sort of universal validity over and against man (e.g., Williams 1970, Keddie 1973). A caveat – reification is a process at both theoretical and pre-theoretical levels, and it must not be looked upon '. . . as a perversion of an originally non-reified apprehension of the social world, a sort of cognitive fall from grace' (Berger and Luckman 1966): it is just that once we reify certain consequences follow. These consequences themselves cannot be judged in terms of an absolute of right or wrong, or good or bad, but only of being more or less efficient for a particular purpose. In the study of the nature of one area of knowledge (linguistics in this case) these results have to be taken into consideration. Reification tends to 'freeze' the underlying approach to a body of knowledge; or in Kuhn's (1970) terms the paradigm is accepted and the ' . . . results gained in normal research are significant because they add to the scope and precision with which the paradigm can be applied'.

We then have an interaction between the nature of scientific research and its learning and teaching processes on the one hand and the objectification and reification of knowledge on the other. This has led to current linguistic theory being, on the whole, formalistic, i.e., concerned with the description and analysis of sets of linguistic forms, linguistically structured and interrelated. Context – the social setting of language and its *raison d'être* – is not ignored in formalistic theory but tends to be introduced in somewhat distant perspective as a point of reference explaining the opposition and groupings of the form. Without in the least denying the absolute value of these rigorous procedures and definitions, this rigour has tended to breed a self-sustained autotropic science. In a more general way this was commented upon by A. N. Whitehead nearly forty years ago:

> My own criticism of our traditional educational methods is that they are far too much occupied with intellectual analysis, and with the acquirement of formalized information . . .
> At present our education combines a thorough study of a few abstractions, with a slighter study of a large number of abstractions. We are too exclusively bookish in our scholastic routines (1933, pp. 284–286).

SOCIAL GRAMMAR AND TRADITIONAL GRAMMAR

We now go on to discuss the differences between my approach and that of traditional linguistics (traditional here having the simple connotation of 'linguistics up to this moment'). First of all I suggest that the difference in approach is between an 'IS' approach, and a 'DOES' approach.[7]

The 'is' approach

This assumes a rather static, one-sided condition of languages, mainly a product put out from an ongoing source such as a speaker or a writer. In this product it discerns levels of linguistic patterning (sounds, grammar, lexis, etc.). With regard to context, the 'is' approach does identify an element of situation which has some sort of function which possibly affects an utterance. Having discerned levels of linguistic patterning these levels are analysed into diverse units (phonemes, morphemes, words, clauses, etc.), and it is the relationships of these forms which are the basic elements of study. Now these are most valuable and necessary procedures without which any study of language is incomplete, and I would suggest they are probably primary in time, not only historically but conceptually. Until this description has been made *and its limitations discovered* it might well have been impossible to produce the complementary description of the 'does' approach. Indeed it might well be that the two approaches may have to be synchronized in the future.

The 'does' approach

This assumes a dynamic (dialectical) two-sided condition of language. That is that language is regarded as a collaborative act requiring interchangeable speaker-hearer relationships, which themselves are the product of complex social relationships which are patterned and organized by ongoing social processes. This approach discovers coordinates of patterning, i.e., that certain linguistic features, often compound features, occur only with specific situational features. Thus we find that the situation gives the pattern to the linguistic features.

It also assumes that all the features of language have to be taken into consideration so that a term such as 'paralinguistic' has to be redefined or may even have become irrelevant. Also in its description of language it assumes a temporal element so that the time continuum may become a factor in description just because society functions inside time.

7. Once again I am indebted to Dr. W. Nash for helping me develop this discussion.

These two approaches start from different points: the 'is' approach starts from the examination of the language in particular instances and, for historical reasons, very often from a print culture. The 'does' approach starts from the nature of the relationship of individuals in cultures and subcultures. Eventually they ought to meet! In fact this dichotomy, I have suggested, is far too sharp; much of the work in language has elements of the two approaches but the greater amount of thought and description has been placed upon the 'is' approach.

The basic difference then is in the material with which we operate. Traditionally it has been the *forms* in the levels of language as perceived by scholars strongly influenced by the Aristotelian and Descartesian traditions. Traditionally '. . . linguistics uses messages as evidence of the structure of the codes in which they are sent' (Greenberg 1968) whereas I suggest that we also look for structure in the society which has created the code in the practice of living. Because speech is both phylogenetically and ontogenetically prior to writing I have concentrated on *parole* rather than *langue;* whilst a written language implies speech always, speech does not imply a written language (Greenberg 1968, p. 22ff.).

AMBIGUITY, THE WRITTEN WORD AND TRANSFORMATIONAL GRAMMAR

In this section I wish to show not only the difference between my approach and that of the more usual linguistics but also to show that certain problems of these linguists are created by their own parameters of operation. As well, it will be seen that their analysis often slips over into the cultural explanation for forms and limitations of forms. It seems sensible to do this with regard to transformational grammar which is dominating the grammatical field at the moment. However this must *not* be taken in any way as a carefully worked out criticism and assessment of transformational grammar; it is utilized only to make some points and to show where my approach is different. It might be that what is said will modify some aspects of this grammar, but that is as far as I would presume to go.

O. Werner (1966) points out that:

The sentences of any language can be arranged into three related sets:

1. Grammatical sentences (as opposed to ungrammatical sentences): the grammar of a particular language enumerates recursively the grammatical and only the grammatical sentences of a language; or, according to a more recent suggestion, the grammar assigns an

automatic index of (un)grammaticality to sentences and generates fully grammatical, as well as ungrammatical sentences (he here cites Katz 1964, Lakoff 1965, Katz and Fodor 1963). The grammar also assigns structural descriptions to sentences.

2. Semantically normal sentences (as opposed to semantically deviant sentences) are a proper subset of all grammatical sentences. The semantic interpretive component of a syntactic-semantic theory (grammar in a very general sense of the term) assigns semantic readings to some but not all grammatical sentences.

3. Culturally appropriate sentences (as opposed to culturally inappropriate sentences) are a proper subset of all sentences which are semantically interpretable (which have semantic meanings).

The ability of a native speaker of a language to distinguish culturally true from culturally false sentences is not part of his linguistic competence but part of his cultural competence. In other words, cultural competence (in a narrow sense) is the native speaker's ability to use language appropriately within the context of his culture. The study of culturally appropriate sentences is the domain of ethnoscience. Thus ethnoscience *ipso facto* concerns language, i.e., how language is used to talk about things.

By subscribing, perhaps unwittingly, to a reified view of grammar Werner has turned grammar upside down and forced a false dichotomy. The argument assumes that the first set, grammatical (and ungrammatical) are an unchanged and unchanging universal whereas this very grammar has grown up in a society and its very grammaticalness is determined by society, by, as I argue later, the group who control power in a society. English grammar has changed over the centuries and is changing at this moment. There are derivative grammars such as the grammar growing up in Nigerian English and the one that has already grown up in American English and Indian English. The apparent underlying deep structure of English grammar is itself a process laid down by centuries of usage in a society. I mentioned above that the grammatical term 'slang' is actually a social judgment on a type of language peculiar to a subculture, as is 'cant'. When we remember the nature of 'in' groups in which these sub-languages develop we realize that one of the functions of languages is to exclude those who are outside - once the outsider learns the slang then a new slang has to be developed. This process of generation, discovering and spreading changes the language and its grammar because so often slang is condemned and indeed given that name because it is ungrammatical! It uses forms and, I suggest, uses forms deliberately that are ungrammatical in Werner's sense in order to maintain an identity and to exclude the world. These 'ungrammatical' forms move into language in general and are eventually accepted. This argument suggests to me that the first set of which the others are sub-sets is the culturally appropriate sentence – 'says who' as a declarative, or even 'says which'; these are acceptable grammatically, if not in some social circles. They are the material on which the grammarian has to work – after all he has denied that grammar is prescriptive.

The quotation above from Werner relates to a discussion:

Examples:
1. 'makes John shoes alligator' is ungrammatical and is clearly not a sentence in English.
2. 'Sincerity makes alligator shoes' although recognizable as some odd form of English is less grammatical than (3) but more grammatical than (1).
3. 'John makes alligator shoes' has two semantic readings: (3a) 'John makes shoes for alligators' which is culturally inappropriate; there are no men in our culture who make shoes for alligators; and (3b) 'John makes shoes out of the hides of alligators' which is culturally appropriate.

Now where is the evidence that (1) is ungrammatical and (3) is grammatical? They are grammatical and ungrammatical when they are compared. They are *different* in word order but that one word order is correct and the other word order is incorrect is not a judgment inherent in the word order but a social judgment made by usage. It is possible to conceive of a subgroup who decide that their 'in' language will have the form 'verb, subject, noun clause' as object, rather than 'subject, verb, noun clause' as object.[8] Then through a cultural change, aided by the mass media, this could penetrate the general language pattern.

There are other points here to look at. There is the distinction between the semantic meanings and the implied ambiguity. First of all any ambiguity lies in the perception of the written word; in the spoken word by use of pause and emphasis and by the appreciation of the cultural rarity of a maker of shoes for alligators, a speaker would draw out the difference. Secondly, the idea of cultural inappropriateness is correct in his society, but I live in a society where shoes are made of all sorts of material, and alligator is just one more; therefore I am transforming, or substituting, just one more material. If, as used to

---

8. I deliberately use the terms 'subject, verb clause, noun clause' as object, purely as a measure of clarity, because the whole nature of what is a sentence is subject to some disagreement and discussion.

happen, one was in a society that made shoes for cows, sheep, ducks and turkeys (Bonser 1970), then (3a) becomes culturally feasible, and I have to distinguish between (3a) and (3b); then I may well start off by using something such as 'shoes for alligators' but quickly use the alternative form of 'alligator (emphasize pause) shoes'. With 'John makes turkey shoes' or 'John makes duck shoes', the ambiguity might well not arise because it would be difficult to make shoes for a man out of a turkey or even part of a turkey! But part of the apparent confusion of 'alligator shoes' is that culturally we are aware that alligator hide might well be as suitable for shoes as any other hide – cow, deer, horse, etc. The added complication of fashion shoes is also a cultural matter.

What I have said in a roundabout way is that much of his argument is cultural – what is grammatically correct is culturally determined; what is semantically correct is culturally determined. Really, all that has been argued is three degrees of discernible cultural influence, perhaps each one a little further back in history or time. But it might well be far more closely connected with power in society. Grammatical universals depend upon cultural and society universals:

'Give us, us teas' – grammatically correct in North England where the personal pronoun 'my' was rarely used; and 'us' is the singular, referring to what is mine.

'Where's our kid' – meaning 'where's my brother'; where 'our' refers to the fact that the 'kid' is shared property with siblings and parents.

However:

'Give us us teas'- is still correctly using the singular because whilst there are many teas available I can only eat one; therefore I ask for 'us tea' for me and 'his tea' for him, and 'her tea' for her, which collapse down into 'us teas' and *not* the southern form 'our teas' – the tea for each of us.

This North country usage is dying out under social pressures of many kinds. However a grammarian has to cope with the fact that many thousands can use and change between

'Give me my tea' and 'Give us us teas'

without any sense of discomfort or any other value judgment. That thousands of others would recognize 'give us us tea' as capable of being generated but make an adverse judgment that it was 'not grammatical' meaning 'it is not my customary usage'. It is also conceivable that there are people who could not generate 'give us us tea'. When we have this situation that a particular construction is capable of generation but not used, and the generation is recognized, we have obviously a social judgment. However if an item is capable of being generated but has not been in some part of a society, this is not an argument for a universal lying 'out there' in language, but a universal being recognized by part of a language speaking group, neither more nor less.

Let us return to 'John makes alligator shoes'. We have, I suggest, two parallel transformations (see schema, next page).

We have the same form derived through two series of experience. It is obvious that in the social setting and in speech we must distinguish between the two meanings. This is done by a particular pattern lying in the so-called paralinguistic features – by the I.S. pattern. *How* this is done is not of present interest. What is of interest is that someone coming new to the situation of these two uses might well struggle with ambiguity until he learnt to distinguish between the two I.S. patterns; part of the descriptive function of a social grammar is to plot these functions and relate them to more general possible confusions. I shall come back to these ambiguities shortly. First one more point to make about Werner's example (2) 'Sincerity makes alligator shoes'. 'Sincerity' is not only a value but it is also a female name, so this is not so much an odd form of English but an odd occupation. Once again Werner's judgment is invalidated because of the confusion of social usage and supposed inherent grammatical objectivity.

With regard to semantics and its place in grammar I can only agree with McCawley when he argues that selectional features are best described in terms of semantic selectional restrictions such as those of Fodor and Katz rather than in the syntactic selection features of Chomsky; however this is not germane to my argument.

I now return more directly to transformational grammar. A full criticism would require more space and time than I have available, but I shall point out a number of weaknesses which show its limitations as far as helping toward a social grammar of English is concerned. They also require consideration by transformationalists as they are directed not so much at the way a machine works as to the nature of the machine.

First there is the assumption that each individual has in him the basic imprint of deep structures that only need bringing out. It should be obvious that the whole of my argument is that language is a social process *as well as* an individual process. In a later chapter I show that items that lie in I.S. in English lie in grammatical forms in some tonal languages. Does this mean that tonal language operators have a different set of deep structures? It is more sensible to assume that deep

A

(a) Shoes are made of durable material; leather is a durable material; hide is a durable material. We have a 'set' of mind; our 'gestalt' of language allows us to consider that anything durable is feasible as shoe material.

SO

(b) 'John makes leather shoes'
'John makes hide shoes'
'John makes wooden shoes'
to a general form
'X makes Y shoes' where X is a person and Y is a durable material.

(c) So when we hear 'John makes alligator shoes' we derive from our general experience of life and language that John makes shoes out of some part of the alligator that is durable.

B

(a) Shoes are made for people mostly to protect their feet.

(b) Similarly shoes are made to protect the hooves of horses

SO

(c) we get a form 'John makes horse shoes.' This is derived from our cultural experience of smiths and farriers. We do not have the idea that shoes are made *out* of horse; we have separated the concept of 'hide' or 'leather' to avoid confusion.

NOW

(d) Given the situation that in England ducks, geese, cows, sheep and, later, turkeys were driven long distances to market, then we have the situation that shoes were made to protect their feet also.

SO

(e) We have the form 'X makes Z shoes' where X is a person and Z means 'animal categories for whom shoes are made.'

structures are implanted by societal processes, i.e., growing up in a society and learning that society's pattern of communication.

Transformational grammar takes as its subject language analysed according to the relationship of forms. It attempts to derive from these relationships general rules which will describe the speaker's competence and that relate signals to the semantic interpretations of these signals. It states that '. . . the theory of generative grammar must provide a general language-independent[9] means for representing the signals and semantic interpretations that are interrelated by the grammars of particular languages (Allen and Van Buren 1971)'. They argue that syntactic descriptions convey information about a sentence beyond its phonetic form and semantic interpretation. The later (1965 version) of Chomsky's theory is summarised by Greene (1972) in the following way:

Components of grammar
1. *Syntactic component* comprising BASE RULES . . . and TRANSFORMATIONAL RULES . . . The LEXICON contains the syntactic, phonological and semantic features of individual words.
2. *Phonological component* comprising PHONOLOGICAL RULES . . .
3. *Semantic component* comprising DICTIONARY ENTRIES for individual words and PROJECTION RULES for combining them according to the syntactic structures of a sentence . . . It is suggested that the dictionary entries should be incorporated into the lexicon as semantic features.

Definition of deep and surface structure
The syntactic component generates a DEEP STRUCTURE and a SURFACE STRUCTURE for every sentence. The deep structure is the output of the base rules (basic syntactic relations and lexical semantic features) and the input to the semantic component; the surface structure is the output of the transformational rules (final order of words and lexical phonological features) and the input to the phonological component.

The social grammarian is concerned with the relationships found in the functions of the elements of language. It is concerned with asking what is the function of those items described by traditional grammar and how are these related to the cultures in which language operates and how these express social relationships.

---

9. 'Language' here must mean language in the sense of English as opposed to French or German, etc.

The transformational grammar separates and classifies separately the syntactic, phonological and semantic features and consequently makes unwarranted assumptions. For example, coming to descriptions of transformational grammar from outside linguistics I was immediately struck by the initial dependence upon the concept of ambiguity and anomaly as a starting point for discussion. But these seem to be less than sensible. Part of the difficulty stems from the difference between what the authors claim and what they actually do. They claim to be discussing utterances but are actually discussing what is visual rather than what is aural.

There is in English a great difference between the spoken and written word going back to the fifteenth century. However this is not just a simple dichotomy; we have a number of discernible gradations of 'written spoken' and 'spoken written' before we get from spoken to written. A moment's reflection on lecturers, either in the lecture room or on the radio or even on T.V. where it is often possible to tell who is actually reading, but reading with feeling; learnt off by heart; or lecturing without reference to detailed written work. Presumably a speech writer is trying to make something written appear to be nearly spontaneous speech. How do we tell these differences? Because we recognise, even if we cannot define, speech as opposed to other varieties through changes in the signal carriers, i.e., lexis, grammar and I.S. These will produce different descriptive grammars; these could start with the social value judgments of 'formal', 'informal', etc. Now the vast majority of the population start off with the spoken word and build up their language competence at all levels on the spoken word. Only later do they master the rules involved in writing and reading (cf. the voluminous work on 'the problems of reading'). I will illustrate one of the complications a little later. Which of these many languages are the transformationalists operating upon? It seems to me that they are using some sort of spoken/written amalgam rather than the ideal speech of the ideal speaker claimed.

AMBIGUITY

In *Problems of Knowledge and Freedom,* Chomsky writes about the ambiguity of the sentence:

'I would speak about such matters with enthusiasm' (Chomsky 1972)

and states categorically that the statement is ambiguous, i.e., that we do not know the meaning; he goes on to suggest that it has two meanings.

There is immediately a logical problem here – if there is this single statement, how do I know that it is ambiguous? Chomsky says that it can mean that my speaking may be enthusiastic or that I would be enthusiastic to speak about such matters. Our common-sense experience of language agrees on the two meanings; the visual examination of the words on the printed page also indicate ambiguity, but how can we have spoken ambiguously? Do we have the sort of double progression as above where I discuss the alligator shoe – with one line having a descent from enthusiasm for speaking, the other a descent from enthusiasm for such matters? This seems unlikely and even ridiculous. However, if we actually try saying this sentence aloud in order to try and show the meanings, we can do it; it is a matter of intonation and stress patterns

'I would speak about such MATters with enTHUSiasm'.[10]
'I would speak about such matters /pause/ with enthusiasm.'

It seems that Chomsky's ambiguity lies in slovenly speech! Or is it that he claims to write about SPEECH, noises, when in fact he writes about writing.[11]

Similarly in Greene's (1972, p.47) work on Chomsky, citing Chomsky's sentence

'The shooting of the hunters was awful'

as ambiguous. Not if we SAY it properly: the ambiguity lies in slovenly speech more than in deriving noun phrases from different kernels. And there is also the logical problem of how do we know it is ambiguous unless we have previous experience of the sentence in non-ambiguous situations?

Again, in *Language and Mind* Chomsky suggests ambiguity in the sentence

'I disapprove of John's drinking' (Chomsky 1968),

where he cannot distinguish between disapproval of John drinking the beer or John's excessive drinking. Here again there is not true ambiguity. It is an artificial one. The confusion is the semantic difference in the two different meanings of 'drinking'. The point of real life, as opposed to an example created to prove a point, is that sentences with ambiguity at the semantic level (and at other levels) rely on being part of a conversa-

---

10. *Cf.* chart page 100 for visual representation.

11. I have had to watch most carefully in this work so as not to use 'what I am saying' when I really mean 'what I am writing'. In the written word we have changed the meaning of 'to say' to mean visual marks.

tion and a social situation which gives clues, contextual clues, to the meaning and also allows for understanding someone else. There is, perhaps, a transformational process, but it is not from just noun clauses, etc. It has a deep social content – but I shall argue this more fully later. But to return to this sentence, there are two further complications which upset Chomsky's analysis of this sentence. The context of the utterance is important because one can have a situation where this sentence has a further meaning or no meaning at all. Given that the 'I' above is an English Muslim, and John is also a Muslim, the reference might not be to alcohol at all but to the drinking of water between sunrise and sunset during Ramadan (the Islamic fast). We actually see a progression, a transformation of the word 'drinking':

originally to satisfy thirst
then   to drink alcoholic beverages
then   to drink alcoholic beverages to excess.

This is surely a social process!

In North Nigeria there is a tribe who were notorious for their heavy and steady drinking (sic); beer was brewed, then everyone – man, woman and child – drank until it was all gone, and then brewed up again; the very idea of disapproval in this case is inappropriate, so 'I disapprove of John's drinking' could be a grammatical sentence in that culture (which uses English extensively), but quite without force.

In *Language and Mind* Chomsky cites:

'I don't like John's cooking any more than Bill's cooking'.

Again the ambiguity is visual. When spoken we can distinguish between two menaings.

'I know a taller man than Bill.'

It depends upon where we place the emphasis. Allen and Van Buren (1971, p. 11) cite:

'They don't know how good meat tastes'.
'What disturbed John was being disregarded bv everyone'.

Fodor and Katz (1964) also have examples:

'I shot the man with the gun'.
'The dark green house is empty'.

Here, once more, the ambiguity is visual and not aural. This draws attention to a serious weakness in transformational grammar: they ignore the *function* of those paralinguistic features intonation, stress, timbre, pause, etc., the most significant being stress and intonation usually working in combination. These I.S. items have to be taken into account for meaning as much as words and word order.

English people, at least, seem to like to utilize as few words as possible or make one collection of phonemes do duty for a number of different things or ideas. They rely consistently and constantly on other factors to give a clear meaning – those factors often include paralinguistic features and the context in which the phoneme is uttered.

A similar discussion met early on in transformation grammar is that of anomaly. Once again the examples used do not support the weight of argument. McCawley (in Bach and Harms 1968) discusses three sentences taken from Chomsky.

1. 'John is as sad as the book he read yesterday'.
2. 'He exploits his employees more than the opportunity to please'.
3. 'Is Brazil as independent as the continuum hypothesis?'

He suggests that there are two lexical items sad_1 and sad_2. Sad_1 meaning 'experiencing sadness, said of a living being'; sad_2 meaning 'evoking sadness, said of an aesthetic object'. He then has a tree diagram which '... could represent any of the four conceivable deep structures, depending upon whether the items labelled *sad* are occurrences of sad_1 or sad_2'.

He argues in detail why all four are anomalous. Despite his careful argument I suggest that there is no anomaly at all. I can conceive, indeed I have conceived, a situation where John has read a book which has had as subject matter material which warrants the description of a sad book (a Victorian novel?) and now in a literary family the unkind brother searching to be different says:

'John is as sad as the book he read yesterday'.

Similarly in (2) we have a rather clever comparison describing someone making a social choice – someone who exploits his employees rather than pleases them.

The third sentence might be anomalous in the quick reading or the generality of conversation. But it could also be a witty response based on the speaker's knowledge of the immediate situation of an argument where his opponent is arguing that the continuum hypothesis is not independent of man, and so the speaker makes the sarcastic comment:

'Is Brazil as independent as the continuum hypothesis?'

Farfetched, but possible, and thus removing the anomaly.

Fillmore (1968) makes a similar mistake with the series:

1. 'John broke the window'.
2. 'A hammer broke the window'.
3. 'John broke the window with a hammer'.

He goes on to say that the subject of (1) and (2) are grammatically different and explains that the combined meaning of the two sentences is not produced by conjoining their subjects. Thus

'John and a hammer broke the window' is unacceptable.

It might be unacceptable to some rule, but it is a perfectly possible sentence in language said by an adult to another adult about the child, a small child, in the situation in which the child has, accidentally, broken the window with a hammer and, in what is a real explanation to the child, has said:

'It was the hammer that broke the window'.

The sympathetic adult says to a third party, partly in extenuation and partly humourously:

'John and the hammer broke the window'.

The point has been made, I trust, without further heaping up of examples. One of the mainstays of transformational grammar seems to be the need to explain ambiguities and anomalies. If utterances and context are taken into consideration, rather than isolated sentences analysed as visual experiences on a page, then much of the analysis seems abortive. However, this is a criticism not so much of the operations but the material upon which the operations work.

A more fundamental limitation is the way they look at language. O. Werner (1966, pp. 43–44) suggests that: 'The sentences of any language can be arranged into three related sets:

(1) Grammatical sentences (as opposed to ungrammatical sentences): the grammar of a particular language enumerates recursively the grammatical and only the grammatical sentences of a language or, according to a recent suggestion, the grammar assigns an automatic index of (un)grammaticalness to sentences and generates fully grammatical as well as ungrammatical sentences. The grammar also assigns structural descriptions to sentences.

(2) Semantically normal sentences (as opposed to semantically deviant sentences) are a proper subset of all grammatical sentences. The semantic interpretive component of a syntactic theory (grammar in a

very general sense of the term) assigns semantic meanings to some but not all grammatical sentences.

(3) Culturally appropriate sentences (as opposed to culturally inappropriate sentences) are a proper subset of all sentences which are semantically interpretable (which have semantic readings).

The ability of a native speaker of a language to distinguish culturally true from culturally false sentences is not part of his linguistic competence but part of his cultural competence. In other words, cultural competence (in the narrow sense) is the native speaker's ability to use language appropriately within the context of his culture. The study of culturally appropriate sentences is the domain of ethnoscience. Thus ethnoscience *ipso facto* concerns language use, i.e., how language is used to talk about cultural things.

To me, in this passage, Werner has turned the argument upside down. By accepting a reified view of the nature of grammar he sees his first set as unchanged and unchanging universals lying outside man as it were whereas this very grammar has grown up in a society, and its very grammaticalness is defined and supported by the power group of the society. English grammar has changed and is changing, not only in England but elsewhere. There are derivative grammars such as the grammar growing up in Nigerian English, those that have grown up in American English and Indian English. The deep structures of English grammar are the result of long social processes laid down by centuries of usage. As society has changed and developed so has language changed and developed with it. Terms such as 'cant', 'slang', 'correct', 'incorrect' are social judgments depending not upon an external authority for value and maintenance but upon social power and usage.

Let us then start not from the analysis of form and attempt to derive deep forms from surface forms on the printed page but start from language as a social function and regard culturally appropriate sentences as the base from which the semantically normal sentence is sanctioned, and then from these two we see that the grammatical sentence is derived.

Very briefly, in support of this, let us look at the growth of language. A child grows up in a net of human relationships inside the family (however defined – it is relevant to suggest that a child growing up in an extended family has a much greater opportunity for observing and identifying the many roles *vis-à-vis* adults, children older, younger and peer group, male, and female and all the permutations possible, than in the nuclear family). These relationships are expressed in language. Certainly in English and in many other languages the first sounds that a child identifies are those covered by the term paralinguistic. Mother uses the words

'What a nasty smelly little child; you ought to be ashamed of yourself',

and the child laughs and gurgles because the tone is reassuring. In his very early life a child is upset by an angry verbal exchange; long before he recognises words he distinguishes anger directed at him and anger directed away at other people. In his early life he hears and sees a whole range of *emotional* relationships expressed largely by I.S., and he sees these in situations of status and solidarity, i.e., authority or non-authority and friendship. He learns, sometimes the hard way, what he can and cannot say, and in what circumstances he can say them. Language is part of human behaviour and is restricted by social conditions as is any other behaviour pattern. What is correct and what is incorrect is not determined by the rules of grammar, as outside and over and away from man, but by structures already developed and changed by society and which can also be changed at the instigation (even the whim) of the power elite in society (this is not necessarily political power).

If we carefully observe the growth of language in a child we see him responding to emotion, either positive self-gratification or negative rebuke, through I.S. patterns. Much of his early language is one word or two words to do with self and his needs. Growth seems to be from crude concepts expressed by nouns and verbs:

'Baby food',
'Mummy come',

working through to more complex relationships, and the introduction of adjectives, adverbs and later the more complex forms of English.

The functional series is emotion, social relations, concrete ideas, abstract ideas. It is from this series, then, that we begin to lay down the regular patterns which we later produce as language and which presumably provide the basis for the generating of all the sentences, etc., which we use. (The desire for regularity and pattern, which seems to be a deep-seated need in man shows itself when the child produces regular past tense forms for irregular verbs; or when he uses forms which bring down a rebuke as unsuitable for use to an adult, or a stranger, but which are a proper pattern between children or inside the family.)

When the child moves into more formal education and learns to write, he learns new conventions of language which are almost completely due to the demands of the printed page. The first is the separation of sounds into words which destroys the basic rhythmic pattern of English. Listen to the early reader saying each word separately, then adding them up and producing whole rhythmic and meaningful patterns.

'Dick-said-that-he-would-come-to-the-party-on-Saturday'

becomes

'Dicksaid thathewouldcometothepartyonSaturday',

with appropriate strong and weak stresses.

The child also has to learn the semantic conventions of the printed page that replace the information carried mainly by I.S. but often by the context of the utterances. Take, for example, the monologue 'John and Marsha' (Freberg) which consists of the repetition of the names one after the other – John 23½ times and Marsha 22 times. It is simply the story of seduction! The story is told by firstly giving a background of soft romantic music – the violin and the organ; it would not have worked with a brass band! Secondly, the tone of voice changes with each repetition of the names.

I made the following notes as a preliminary to making a written description of the record.

Name John said by female	*Name Marsha said by male*
1. welcome surprise	pleasure and welcome
2. deeply affectionate	deeply affectionate response
3. questioningly (implying some approach by male)	hesitantly but continuing approach
4. intake of breath then surprise and indignation	complex of reassurance, coaxing, and seeking approval to continue.
5. intake of breath, voice full of happiness	intensity and passion
6. sharp intake of breath, choked voice but with happiness	drawn-out word full of love and affection.
7. sniff, as (6) but more so.	an 'mmmmmm' of satisfaction
8. sniff, lovingly drawing attention and so on	climax of satisfaction

To make a running written description requires a very good technique of written English: 'We have here the two voices, one of a man, John, and the other of a woman, Marsha. They are relating to each other just through the use and repetition of their partner's name. The whole of the repetitions are set against a background of soft romantic music played mostly on a violin and a little on the organ. Firstly the woman says her partner's name in a welcoming but somewhat surprised tone. He responds similarly but with less surprise and a little hope. She repeats his name in tones of deep affection which draws out an equally affectionate response. Obviously he makes some physical approach, and she replies questioningly which provokes him into repeating her question but also with the indication that he is going to continue. There is a sharp intake of breath from Marsha, and she sharply calls his name with surprise and indignation. John is not dismayed and replies by saying her name in a complexity of reassurance, coaxing and seeking approval to continue. She obviously encourages him because there is a sharp intake of breath followed by a voice full of happiness. Equally happy his voice contains also an intensity of passion. Once again Marsha's choked, happy voice is preceded by a quickly indrawn breath. John, on the other hand, replies with a long drawn out loving utterance of her name. Marsha then sniffs and immediately follows up with a more intense version of her previous "John". He can only respond by a "mmmmmmmmmm" of satisfaction. "Sniff" goes Marsha and calls his attention (as if it were needed!) by using a drawn-out loving tone. This provokes a satisfied "Marsha" ' etc.

This shows, I think, the tremendous amount of written verbal dexterity necessary to describe the I.S. patterns of the spoken word which have much to do with emotion. If I wanted to *tell* you about this and if I had any sense, I would either learn it by heart, have a portable tape recorder or encourage you to listen to it. The whole of the previous paragraph is demanded by the printed requirements and requires someone experienced in writing to do it.

In the written word we go through the exercises of turning direct speech into indirect speech. Whereas in conversation we either paraphrase or quote directly. There is a whole vocabulary range and grammatical construction demanded by the written word and adverbs of manner such as 'laughingly', 'quietly' which describe voice condition. These adverbs in direct speech are found in I.S.

In present transformational practice it is impossible to do the transformational processes on the original repetition of names, but it would be possible on either my notes or the long verbal description. It is not my place to explicate either the problem of where did the deep structures come from or where did they go. However, I would suggest that before we can do any transformation we have to start in the reverse order of Werner's list. Before we can discuss and attempt to generate deep syntactic structures which we can label grammatical forms, we have to find prior sociolinguistic structures involving first emotion, then social relationships, then the lexical expressions and finally grammatical expressions.

In all the 'ambiguous' sentences looked at previously the information is there in the spoken I.S. pattern; in the written word it is found in semantic and grammatical[12] structures. A simple analysis using transformational techniques has ignored these, probably for two reasons:

1. The operators have never clearly decided whether they were operating on the spoken or the written word.
2. The operators assume, for historical reasons, that the items for analysis are to be found in the relationships of form.

The problems caused by the former I have already outlined. The latter is equally unfortunate. If as I argue language is the product of individuals working in groups, then it is possible, indeed has happened, that different groups will use different physiological processes to show the many different social intentions which have to occur in the communication process. This means that forms may be used differently in different societies – to search for universals in forms and relationships of forms is logically impossible. However, as language is a product of society there may be a possibility of finding universals in social and individual relationships which operate across societies. Our first analysis must be upon these; these are the deep structures on which different societies build different grammars. As far as English is concerned, they are going to be about two sets of transformations – one dealing with the spoken word, the other with the written word. But these deep structures are going to be found not in form as such but form as determined by socially determined relationships.

GRAMMAR AS FORMS

In discussing the aims of linguistic theory, Greene (1972, p. 25) makes the following statement:

> This is simply making explicit an assumption that underlies even the most old-fashioned 'prescriptive' grammar. Prescriptive grammars are those which attempt to lay down some standard of correct usage, such as the 'Queen's English', as opposed to modern descriptive grammars which are concerned with language as it is actually spoken. However, in both cases *anyone who follows the rules of the grammar will produce sentences that are considered correct by the grammar and*

---

12. It is interesting that I use 'grammar' in two ways. In this instance it is the traditional and popular one of word arrangement. Other times it is used in the more special sense of a particular view of language.

will avoid incorrect utterances not allowed by the grammar (my emphasis).

We must not assume that the rules of the grammar lie 'out there' and that they are independent of social processes and, ultimately, social control. 'Correct' and 'incorrect' are socially and temporally bound and are always at the mercy of social change. The 'rules' of any grammar cannot solely be derived from the study of the form of the sentence; they have to take note of social realities. Transformational grammarians acknowledge this, but it is so easy to unconsciously assume that any particular rule or set of rules exists out there. We seek for universals, but there is a limit to the search when we concentrate on relationships in form and ignore the relationships in the society which produces the forms. If we take the sentence:

'Silent as a banana',

this can be, in transformational terms, rightly said to be a deviant combination of selectional features. But only as long as the deviancy is socially approved. The teacher meeting this sentence in a child's writing might well be pleasantly surprised and say 'What an interesting new metaphor!' There are two further points arising out of this. The first I will deal with briefly; the second is germane to the whole concept of social grammar.

First, then, is the suggestion that as English (as opposed to American English or Nigerian English, etc.) has different forms in England due to differing social and cultural milieus, we may finish up with not just one transformational grammar system but a main system with variations according to different sections of society each with its own rules. There is a limit to the universal rules which can be formed from the study of form, because form itself is different according to its sources in different forms and sub-forms of society.

Secondly, transformational grammar is, at least to some degree, a second stage of analysis. Take a sentence we have looked at before:

'John broke the window'.

The analysis has made an assumption, an unwarranted assumption that this is a simple statement of fact. But it can, of course, be a question, an exclamation of horror, a cry of derision. Before one can discuss transformations I suggest that the prior decision has to be analysed. In the second part of this study I go on to look at the social function of I.S. in English and also develop the idea that in certain languages the function found in I.S. in English is found in grammatical features.

Chomsky (1972, pp. 22ff.) says that we learn words by exposure to their use; this is of course true, but it is inadequate. We learn their use and also when *not* to use them in social situations. As I show later, the learning of words is embedded in our status situation, our solidarity situation and our emotional state. Long before a child develops vocabulary he is aware of a range of emotions and status. He learns love and its expression – anger, domination, and other social relationships – as part of his socializing process as well as part of his language learning process. Words come from a whole net or web of relationships and like the surveyor we need triangulation points to find ourselves. To find these triangulation points I am looking in the social relationships as they appear in language.

Take the grammatical class 'adverbs of manner' supposedly a description of form but actually a description of social and personal behaviour. Consider the following:

1. He said questioningly, 'John broke the window'.
2. He said sarcastically, 'John broke the window'.
3. He said with horror, 'John broke the window'.
4. He said threateningly, 'John broke the window'.

'Questioningly', 'sarcastically', 'with horror', 'threateningly' all deal with attitudes towards persons. These words are mainly, if not exclusively, literary words; that is, they have developed with writing to give visual expression to those attributes normally carried in I.S. features in English. They are a product of the considerable difference between the spoken word and written word in English.

In many English language examinations there used to be, and very often still is, the exercise known as 'put into direct speech' or more usually 'Put into indirect speech the following passage'. This is for most people purely a written procedure; it has been produced by the great need of written English to show the non-verbal communication patterns of the spoken word.

If you listen to conversation patterns we rarely use the paraphernalia of the written indirect speech form. We *either* use direct speech taking the part of each speaker in turn, i.e., I do not report by saying 'He said threateningly "what are you doing here?" ' but I actually produce the quotation using a threatening tone of voice, and so on through the whole episode: *or* we just give a summary of the whole episode – we paraphrase!

In discussing the passive, Chomsky (1972, pp. 31ff.) is concerned with form, but the use of passive is far more concerned with social matters, e.g., attention-drawing or focus shifting. Take Chomsky's examples:

'I believe the dog is hungry'.
'The dog is believed to be hungry'.

We are drawing attention, by the passive, to the dog being hungry (Quirk et al. 1972, p. 57) or it might be a stylistic device to avoid monotony of the active voice. It is also involved with status and other status situations. The passive is also the disassociation from the personal, and, because of this lack of the personal, it is in some mysterious way supposed to be less subjective and more objective and thus more suitable, for example, for academic texts. This is an arbitrary social judgment. But to return to a Chomskian analysis I would suggest that his analysis is incomplete and runs into difficulties because of the priority of the social determinant in the material he is trying to handle.

It should be obvious that this priority of status, emotion and solidarity applies to the other authors I have discussed. To give one example only, McCawley (in Bach and Harms 1968, pp. 155ff.) discusses Austin's 'performative verbs' and Ross's modifications. He discusses and gives the three for an imperative – 'open the door'. But the imperative is only one meaning of this form: it can be modified in writing by adverbs of manner. In communication it may well be a question or rejection, etc., depending upon information given in the I.S. pattern and the social context.[13]

The transformational grammarians' position may be summarized as follows: 'Henceforth language shall no longer be regarded as a corpus of utterances *per se* but rather as the abstract system of rules which underlies these utterances' which for me is all right as far as it goes, which is not very far because it immediately poses the question as to where these rules are to be found. Chomsky (1968, p. 81) suggests that they lie in the mind, that 'language has no existence apart from its mental representations' and ' . . . it is fair to suppose that the major contribution of the study of language will lie in the understanding it can provide as to the character of mental processes and the structures they form and manipulate'.

I suggest that these rules are found not in the mind alone but in the human mind as a product developed in the social situation and that we have to look also in the social situation for these rules – that man is also an emotional creature and that to some degree his expression of emotion is limited or permitted by his social situation and here again we must search for some of our rules.

---

13. The whole of this argument is closely related to grammatical fit; cf. page 23 above.

There is the further question of the 'structures' that mental processes form and manipulate. As I understand this it is the forms of sentences, the normal material of linguists; I have already suggested that this is inadequate because it leads to definitions of some communication processes as paralinguistic, which in some groups of languages are handling what is linguistic data in English.

CHAPTER II

Social Grammar of Language

> Social factors not only influence the competence
> of individual speakers and the status of function-
> al language varieties; there is also a social comp-
> onent at the heart of grammar (D. Hymes 1971,
> p. 8).

This chapter[14] falls into three parts. Part 1 looks briefly at some aspects of the growth of language. This leads on to Part 2 where I suggest that there are three relationships from society which can be used as a basis for analysis in social grammar. This leads to Part 3 where I argue the need for a description of language according to function rather than form because form has lost its original social meaning.

Part 1: Some aspects of the growth of language

There is a voluminous literature in the field of the growth of language covering the work of my first professor, M.M. Lewis, via Piaget through to collections of essays such as Hymes (1971). However I want to draw attention to one aspect of the growth of language that has been neglected – that of the *development* of the expression of emotions and social status in society as it refers to language.

As far as I have been able to find, there is no literature on this, and what I have to say is built upon my own observations and that of students (many of whom are married men and women) and friends who have either agreed that my observations have accorded with their own experiences or have offered instances agreeing with mine or deliberately observed their off-spring and those of friends over periods of about a year. I started from a logical deduction from some premises. First, most people recognize the

14. This chapter can be read before, after or alongside Chapter III.

emotional state of others in the social situation and generally realize whether any particular emotion is directed toward them or some other person. Secondly, we are all aware that there are times when we can and cannot indulge in an emotional outburst. These are part of our general social competence. Thirdly, in the latter case the situations vary from society to society and from subculture to subculture. This suggested to me that both emotional expression and social awareness, to state the obvious, are learnt.

When I came to examine what was happening to children, I realized that this particular aspect of language started quite early in the child's life. Particularly when I realized that emotion in English is largely carried in those paralinguistic features I refer to under the symbol 'I.S.'. Within a few days of birth, maybe even hours, the mother is saying words but also making 'nonsense' sounds to the child as a reassuring activity. These are usually associated with comforting physical reactions. One definition of a baby is that a baby is an alimentary canal open at both ends. This requires a lot of work for a mother who is constantly removing sources of discomfort and producing states of satisfaction. We do not need to enter into any of the psychological descriptions and theories but need only note that usually this mothering activity is accompanied by a great deal of communication. A most interesting factor is that, perhaps not early with the first child, but often with second and subsequent children, the *words* of the mother do not coincide with either the physical intention or the *I.S.* used.

'Who's mother's filthy smelly little beast then?'
'Who's a horrible little stinky poo making more work?'

says mother, busily the while removing the offending nappy, cleaning up the disaster area and smiling, and often stopping to smile and fondle the child. According to the linguistic competence of the mother, and perhaps social class, the language used might be referred to as 'foul' or 'obscene'. The mother who lovingly cares for her child and at the same time might well say:

'Come on you fucking little bastard; let's get your fucking arse clean'

by her underlying I.S. pattern is suggesting love and care.

Having watched mothers, and mother surrogates, caring for children in a number of countries and a number of language situations, I suggest that some of this paralinguistic content is physiologically based. That anger, for instance, is associated with physiological changes that affect the vocal cords and breathing is obvious. But what is equally obvious when one takes part is that certain sounds – 'cooing' sounds – reassure babies from many different language groups. However, this is an aside.

To return to my main argument, the child is surrounded by sounds and actions showing a whole range of social relationships. If you watch a child carefully you will see that at first it is liable to cry at any very loud sound, but it adapts to both sound level and type of sound. A child living on a busy road is not disturbed by traffic noises but might well be constantly upset by country noises. Within limits, familiarity and regularity seem to be the important factors. But quite quickly a child seems to distinguish the direction of sound, particularly I.S. patterns suggesting emotion. Within certain levels it can distinguish between anger directed at itself and anger directed perhaps at the husband or another child. Certainly, actual level is a factor here. Though I do not think there is an absolute decibel level above which a child is frightened, there is more likely a base level, of complexity too great to quantify, from which a child works. In my experience and that of my informants, this coarse discrimination is true for expressions of love, amusement and impatience.

As a child becomes less passive, in the sense of movement and exploration, he is surrounded – according to his family situation – with a whole complex of social attitudes expressed in language situations. He sees and hears mother being angry with brothers, sisters and himself but never with father. Or he experiences the converse. The point I want to establish and emphasize is that a child is not just building up a whole vocabulary or a pattern of grammatical forms, he is building up a whole pattern of social language responses. As with the rest of language, what he recognizes is probably much greater than what he can produce. Also I think it is very important to remember that this process is going on from a child's earliest moments, and I suggest that the emotional communication precedes verbal communication, whilst the social relationship communication pattern is learnt, certainly coterminous with, and perhaps slightly before, the vocabulary and grammatical features. It is also important to remember that semantic items and the construction of the language are set in a matrix of these emotional and social patterns. Thus the child learns not just an unemotional 'the dog's on the mat' but an angry statement or a surprised [15] statement or an incredulous statement. Even simple commands are couched in a variety of emotions and social situations. This can have quite startling consequences in later life. About seven years ago I was asked to a local school to help with the problems caused by five West Indian girls who were causing chaos in the third year. They were about fourteen years old and had recently arrived in England from Jamaica. With a Jamaican teacher on a course at the university, I went down to investigate. The

---

15. *Cf.* my comments about adverbs of manner; they are also relevant to adjectives of manner to some degree.

youngsters were ignoring all commands, shouting and generally doing what they wanted, to everyone's discomfort. They were not doing damage but just stopping all work. After some time we discovered that they were from a remote corner of the island with their homes running parallel to but at a fair distance from the communal taps. The children played by the taps and the mothers shouted at them from a distance. The general culture is highly authoritarian with a lack of polite forms when speaking to children, with the strongly authoritarian falling tone of English. These girls were conditioned to shouted orders in a highly authoritarian pattern and were just not hearing the normal school language pattern (cf. page 24 above; this sequence would have been impossible with these girls). We then had three or four weeks of teaching these girls the possibility of other patterns of orders; not only had they to actually hear the words, etc., but they had to learn to distinguish the social context in which the words were uttered and the I.S. pattern in which they were embedded. One had the somewhat comical, but rather disturbing, situation of a university lecturer and English women teachers standing three or four feet from girls, shouting at them at the top of their voices!

Again, not so lang ago, I was asked to help with a child of nine. He was brought to school by mother as the family had removed to the area after the beginning of term. After mother had gone he was taken to his classroom and introduced to the teacher. From then on there was a most strange situation. Unless the boy was actually *led* from place to place by teacher, or told by other children, he not only did not obey instructions but did not understand them. His mother was eventually asked for help. She came to the school and smilingly said that all that was wrong was that the teachers did not know how to handle him! She asked what they wanted and they said:

'Well, he's standing there; ask him to sit down.'

The mother went across to him, smacked him across the face, said very authoritatively 'Sit down' and the child sat down, apparently quite happy.

'There' said mum, 'when you want anything, just give him a smack across the face, and he'll be all right' and went off home.

What does the teacher do now? In fact you have, in my terms, a good example of status conditioning. In a status-inferior position this child was cued by a smack. However in the status-equal situation the child responded to normal conversational procedure. In other children he was aware of a variety of command forms. So by working through the children, by addressing the child indirectly for a long time, it was possible to teach this child another set of patterns for a status-inferior situation. I have no doubt that this child was developing, as we all do, a number of situations for language response which include not only responses to a group-status situation but an individual-status situation, i.e., the child cited had built up a general adult/child situation response from his mother and now is learning a teacher/child response, but also has to generalize not only to his class teacher but to teachers as a group. This particular case has left me frustrated because, for obvious reasons, I cannot follow up and study the child in various situations.

To return to my main theme, then. I have said that a child learns not just statements but statements with emotional bases and in social settings. Just as a child finds order in grammar, so he finds order in society. He relates the order in one to the order in the other. But much of his language training is actually social training. To describe this I obviously oversimplify; the process in any particular case must be highly complex, but we can abstract, as it were, a simplified statement of procedure. Let us continue to concentrate on anger. The child is the recipient of anger. First he is aware of it as undifferentiated sound; he becomes more aware of anger associated with words and patterns of words. But he also becomes aware of situations in which anger can and cannot be shown. For example, his mother and father can be angry with him, but he cannot be angry with them. They can be angry with his little brother, but he cannot be – not when mother and father can find out! He can show his anger about Mrs. F. in her absence but not in her presence. Mother is angry with him openly in some situations but hides it in others and shows it after the guests have gone. It is obvious that I am talking about the growth of language competence. Unfortunately for my purposes the bulk of studies of the difference of speech in children are concerned not with linguistic competence or sociolinguistic competence[16] but frequency of structure, as in the works of Bernstein and his colleagues in the U.K. Psycholinguistics has been concerned with the mental processes by which language grows in the child which, again, does not help me.

The material which grammarians, sociolinguists and psycholinguists so use is derived from a study of form. The whole function of this part of the study is to show and to emphasize that these forms are

---

16. When we talk of competence we must, as Ervin-Tripp (in Alatis 1970. pp. 37–38) points out, distinguish between two meanings of competence: 'One concerns basic rules which everyone masters who is a member of a community: if you fail you are ignorant, an outsider, a social bore, or a bit strange. The other type of competence involves ranked skill where the criteria of success can be formally defined but where success is beyond the capacity of some individuals'. Both types of competence are discussed in sociolinguistic literature, but Bernstein, for example, is concerned more with the first type than the second, commenting on two classes in a community.

embedded in forms determined by emotional and status concepts which lie in the society. In the study of language they require a prior study because not only can they alter the nature of the form but also condition the description of the form and its function.

The whole corpus of literature discussing, for example, significant others or primary and secondary socialization does not help me to establish my theory. On the contrary, I suggest that the concepts I have developed contribute to these views of the nature and growth of language in children. As Casagrande points out, Hallowell in 1955 drew

> ... attention to the *generic* function of language in providing linguistic means of orientating the individual to the culturally constituted world he apprehends... [Hallowell] calls attention to language universals other than the pronominal systems that serve to orient the individual in a self-other dimension (in Greenberg 1963, pp. 226-227).

It is then suggested that kinship terms as a subset of status terms is not enough and that these are particular examples of a *relationship,* and that status implies a whole range of social controls over language expression. I also suggest that the expression of emotion is a social universal which allows a person to locate himself and that both emotion and status are at least contemporaneous and might well be prior to semantic representation in the language situation.

One last point to which I wish to draw attention is the prescriptive action of society in language growth. Briefly the subculture in which we grow up defines the standards that are proper for that subculture. The family is often referred to as a primary socializing institution, and the family gives a first language situation. The school, being a secondary socializing institution particularly where education is thought of as a means of social change, then has a function as a secondary social control over language. Tremendous concern has been expressed about children's linguistic ability (or lack of it), and programmes such as 'Head Start' in the U.S.A. and the E.P.A.'s in the U.K. have been set up to deal with what was conceived of as language deprivation, though doubt is being cast upon the analysis of the problem. It is irrelevant to my purposes as to whether the language difference lies in a contrast between two language subsystems or the same system with a gradation of lack of ability. I would suggest that by utilizing a social grammar analysis – certainly contemporaneously with a linguistic analysis or even slightly prior to it – we may well be able to define the problem a little more clearly and also suggest other answers.

Our social role as perceived by ourselves – in contrast to its perception by others – is shown in language concerning judgments, such as:

'Isn't he vulgar?'
'He's a snob'
'How dare you speak like that'
'Don't be impertinent'
'Who does she think she is, Lady Muck?'

Part 2: Status, solidarity and emotion[17]

> That there exist general designs for languages and
> cultures is a belief frequently affirmed by anthro-
> pologists and linguists if seldom demonstrated in
> detail (Casagrande, in Greenberg 1963, p. 221).

Casagrande (op. cit. p. 223) then suggests of other contributors to the symposium that their explanations for the occurrence of universals in both anthropology and linguistics are couched in underlying determining factors rather than in the phenomena of language or culture *per se*. My theory is that we can find three fundamental factors in the concepts of status, solidarity and emotion. But a word first about meanings. I shall be using these words and others such as 'role' and 'stratification' in their ordinary everyday meanings which can usually be gained from the context in which I use them. However, having approached the systematic formulation of my theory more from sociology and social anthropology, I suspect that the underlying set of my mind will lead to formulations of definitions which derive from these areas of knowledge.

These concepts of status, solidarity and emotion I conceive as relationships operative over a large area of language study. These relationships are rooted in society and the individuals' reaction to society and individuals' reactions to each other in all sorts of groups and individual situations. Now we are involved in a communication difficulty; because a book is linear, I must talk about these items one after the other, but they all interact and affect each other. A visual model would be where status is a vertical axis, solidarity is a horizontal axis and the relationship of these two to each other determines what can be said to whom and by whom; emotion is at right angles to the other in the third plane interacting with the other two, very often its position in the language determining process being governed by the other two, but at the final crunch emotion is the overriding determinant.

17. A brief outline of this section originally appeared in Grayshon (1975b).

I shall first discuss *status,* which is fundamental, more easily defined, initially in the language situation more influential and simplifies the analysis of the other two. Status has to do with vertical language, the social power bases of language which often dictate 'correct' style, 'rightness', etc., and the authority for many of the social descriptions of language which masquerade as objective linguistic descriptions.

Then *solidarity* (sometimes referred to as social distance) which through concepts such as friendship moderates the determining process of status. This is an area, as will become obvious, where there are many loose ends; I am not yet sure whether it is that which is left after status and emotion have been dealt with or whether it has a much more definite outline.

Finally I shall discuss *emotion.* This can be the overriding factor in the language situation. I am interested in its two functions of joining or rejecting in human situations. Whilst normally status determines what emotions are publicly expressible, nevertheless extreme emotional situations can override all other considerations. Solidarity requires a positive emotional quality which can then control and modify negative emotional qualities.

These three relationships underline many complex social relationships and are determining forces so often in the who-can-say-what-to-whom-and-in-what-circumstances game which we call life. I am using these to give form, perhaps a crude form at this stage of the proceedings but nevertheless a clear and definite form, to the social context of language and thus to language itself. The relationship of these to the more usual linguistic descriptions of language is taken up in a later section where I show that they move across the different linguistic descriptions in different language groups.

STATUS

This is not a fixed position in society but a relationship between two people or groups of people or language groups. There are two basic situations, that of superior-inferior and inferior-superior. The relationship between equals could be status, but it is, I suggest, the link between status and solidarity. A superior is the person or group who is in a position of power and therefore has more say in decisions as to what language may be used. This power must not be conceived of as only political power; it is power in its widest terms. In our reality maintenance we utilize language to maintain our position, to agree our roles *vis-à-vis* others, to estimate our positions in society and to change and improve our position. Status is a basic relationship in all this activity. Initially high status, i.e., a great social distance, either formally or informally determines what can be said by whom to whom. *The general rule is that the superior has more language choices than the inferior and that the actual choices available are both socially and individually controlled by the superior.* In the highly authoritative and structured subculture of the army, a whole range of language performances is under the control of the superior. Indeed, before that the whole business of verbal communication is under the control of the superior:

'Permission to speak, Sir.'
'Not granted.'

And that is the end of that. Even when permission is granted, the actual form of words, the whole communication pattern remains under the control of the superior (Grayshon 1973, pp. 40ff.). The desire to disagree, to contradict, requires a whole complex of linguistic features which allow the listener (the superior) to determine that the speaker (the inferior) is sufficiently respectful, or dutiful.

'Sir, with due respect, sir, I venture to suggest, sir, that perhaps, conceivably, your suggestion might be capable of modification.'

The observers from the same society will be making value judgments. Perhaps from the superior's equals, comments about how respectful, how good, etc. From the inferior's equals, comments about how well George is handling the old man; from the inferior of the inferior perhaps comments about smarmy bastards. However, with regard to the latter it is both socially and personally inadvisable that the middle-ranking speaker hears the inferior talking about smarmy bastards! This nicely illustrates the point of relative status.

Now just as a sergeant is inferior in an individual sense to his captain, so the class non-commissioned officer is inferior as a group to the class commissioned officer. This is an institutional situation. This division between superior and inferior follows throughout the whole of society. In a highly authoritative society with great social distance, a whole language area might be denied to a section of the population and a whole area of language not used by another. In mediaeval England, the nobility and baronage did not even bother to learn the language of the lower class, and their communication was almost completely one-way, and then confined to orders. Even when there was a community of language, what the lower class could say was determined by the nobility and baronage. 'Insolence' is as much a description of 'polite' language as of 'rude' language in certain social situations.

I suggest that these social aspects of language affect etymological structures and development. Here is a specific case:

The transformation of etymology by Neogrammarian linguistics can be illustrated by these two sequences (Ross, A.S.C. Etymology with special reference to English. London, Deutsch. 1958)

1. 1 – E*gʰōus→Common Germanic *kwōz→Old English cū→Modern English 'cow'

2. 1 – E*gʰōus→Oscan bōs→ [by borrowing] Latin bōs, accusative bōvem → [by the accusative stem] Anglo-Norman bōef → [by borrowing] Middle English bēf → Modern English 'beef'

These are etymologically "sames". Yet in English, as is well known, "cow" and "beef" are not the same. No folk-etymology of the two words would turn up a suggestion more apparently improbable at first sight (Ardener 1971, p.223)

Now when considering status in language in a wider sense, we see that these two words represent the same animal in two different social situations. 'Beef' is the superior situation; the animal is now dead and ready for eating at the table of the social superior with the dominant language. He refers to his food in that part of Middle English derived from Norman French. However, the living animal is looked after by the inferior, whose word for this particular beast in Middle English is presumably derived from the Old English and the inferior Saxon language of the conquered tribes. Similarly the other food words mutton/sheep; pork/pig; veal/calf.

These other areas, where the status influence of the users of words affect the meanings, could be investigated for their influence upon etymology. For example, in engineering the protuberances on many items are referred to as 'lugs', certainly the North Country for 'ears' – perhaps our rude mechanics, as they became more skilful and inventive, took their particular brand of English to produce much of our engineering nomenclature, rather than the nobility and gentry who normally kept themselves apart from this type of work. However, this is in a sense an aside, but it does illustrate the importance of status in discussing language, and also it contributes to the view of its universality.

Status is not necessarily overt. In the discussion of classroom language above, the superiority of the teacher was hidden initially in the language used, but the point to note is that the teacher, the superior, determined the situation and the language usage. The appearance of equality does not necessarily mean equality at the choice of either party. It is common in the American, more than the English, situation for Christian names or initials to be used instead of titles of rank or superiority:

'Yes, George' instead of 'Yes, Sir';
'O.K., J.C.' instead of 'Very good, Sir'.

This is not status equality. The norm has been set by the superior, who *insists* upon Christian names. Our observer watching, and more sensibly for our purposes listening, is rarely in doubt as to who is actually the superior. The information for drawing this conclusion I discuss in a later section.

The actual language components giving the information about the status situation may well be rather coarse, and an individual's performance may well depend upon his appreciation of the social context. Vickers (1955, pp. 48–49) points out that in the early days of the National Coal Board when opinions, orders and information began to fly up and down these newly improvised channels, everyone concerned found at first a curious difficulty in making himself understood. In this complex management situation with personnel drawn from private industry (which comprised many firms of different size and management technique) and the civil services, those fixed points of status (and solidarity as I hope to show later) have vanished, and new ones were not yet fixed. The individual was unable, linguistically speaking, to know which of the grammatical forms he should use to give an order, e.g.,

'Would you be so kind as to . . .'
'I think that would be the best thing to do . . .'
'Perhaps you had better do it that way . . .'
'Oh, why don't you do that . . .'
'That's the easiest . . .'
'Do that!'

Which of these is an order, which is a request, depends not upon the grammatical form but upon the relative status of speaker and listener. Meaning, in this and many other situations, is largely a function of choice amongst permissible alternatives, and what is permissible is in the first instance determined by status.

We listen to a verbal exchange between child and parent, and we eventually *say* 'What a spoilt child'. We are making a social judgment upon the family situation and deciding that the parent has abdicated its high status situation in favour of the child.

Referring back to Barth's paper (1966) he basically is dealing with a series of status situations:

(a) The general ship situation is that the Captain is autocratic, but
(b) because there is a solidarity situation, i.e., the crew have contracted with him and are at this level his equals and
(c) once the boats have been lowered, the netboss takes over.

Barth argues that these relationships have to be worked out in a series of transactions. As a social grammarian I am interested in the communication factors that help in this matter. Or from a different point of view, I am interested as an observer in listening to the language and observing the behaviour of the participants and from my previous knowledge of the language infer the status relationships of the participants.

Thus we can say that by being quiet and conversing only with each other they respect the skipper as skipper, but by being on the bridge they are also making the point that they are only in a voluntary and contractual relationship with the skipper. *Or* we can ask ourselves questions such as:

'Are the fishermen being respectful by being on the bridge?'
'What is their relationship to the skipper?'

Similarly with the relationship of the netboss to the crewmen, there is a contractual status-superior relationship that is effective only in the circumstances of the operating of the boats. To distinguish between the solidarity situation of equality on board ship as opposed to the status situation in the boats, the netboss has two distinct language patterns. The first is joking and argumentative and 'gives off evidence of inspired guesswork, flair and subtle sensing' (Barth 1966, p.8), whilst the second is '. . . an institutionalized [sic] pattern of gross and continual cursing and assertion of authority on his part'. I would like much more information about the actual language involved. Just how is the cursing interpreted as showing authority in this situation? Just how is the verbal part of the assertion of authority interpreted? What factors of semantic and grammatical and paralinguistic information are utilized and what is their relationship to each other?

May I emphasize the importance of primary socialization in the family with regard to status. As I pointed out in Part 1, the child is surrounded by status situations which are reflected in the language situation. If the family is highly authoritative with a very clear hierarchical structure and the minimum of verbal play, then the child is learning that, being an inferior, silence is golden. He also learns just what language patterns are permitted to him as an inferior and makes value judgments when he balances the consequences of verbal actions, i.e., a child may well 'cheek' his mother but not his father because the response of the mother to the child's utterance is one that the child can cope with whilst the father's response might well be more violent. The observer of these behaviours is either the 'involved' observer who is making social value judgments on the child's language, such as:

'What a cheeky child'

or the social grammarian who is asking what speech factors and social context allow the value judgments to be made and, who, having found a pattern in some social situations, can then move to another situation and make judgments about the relative status of the participants, including the 'involved' observer.[18]

The linguistically adept can actually assert his position as a superior even though socially he might be in an inferior position. Some comedians claim that they learnt joking behaviour as a defence against bullying, thus as it were reducing the status gap between them and the tormentor. In the institutionalized situation of the Royal Navy there was the incident where a C.P.O. instructor was reflecting long and loud about the incompetency and inefficiency of the squad, in the time-honoured method of reducing the squad to obedience and humility. At the height of the diatribe, in a small pause, came a voice from the back row:

'Oh, what an ogre!'

said in a 'refained' voice. There was a moment's pause, and the whole squad dissolved in laughter. By using a particular type of voice and a carefully chosen word, the whole attempted dominance of the squad was lost, and one somewhat insignificant man had asserted himself. For the social grammarian, why does that type of voice, with that particular semantic choice, have that particular social effect?

I pointed out in Chapter 1 that the reification of language has resulted in the view that certain social descriptions of language were somehow eternal laws. This has happened in the academic world; sociologists dealing with the sociology of knowledge have pointed out that the choice of articles for journals may be determined other than by objective criteria (Crane 1967, pp. 195–201) and that book reviews also may be less than objective (debate in *Journal of Health and Social Behaviour* 2 (4), 1970; pp. 327–329).

When we come to definitions dealing with style, we are looking at status

---

18. 'Involved' here I think of as describing those observers who are part of a culture as opposed to the anthropologist, for example, who is 'outside' the situation.

situations. My argument is briefly that the social activity of academic research has built a power basis from which it originally determined that work should be presented in a form which emphasized the objective nature of the knowledge. Because of the strength of the natural sciences, the view that anything of a personal nature was suspect because it is 'subjective' has informed the whole field of research. Allied, I suspect, with a modesty (or pseudo-modesty) that 'I' should not appear, the use of the passive, the third person 'one', the royal 'we' (which for some reason I cannot suggest is less subjective than 'I'), a style has developed. There is also the general view that the well-educated use a style that is clearer, just because they are well educated. This is just not necessarily so (cf. Doke 1954, p. 44). Gradually the reification of a particular style has given it a sanctity which allows it not only to exist on its own, but to have an existence, an aura of sanctity, which in some mysterious fashion envelops any work written in this style with a special virtue, even if, as we are so often aware, the resultant publication is turgid, boring and laborious. Now the determinants of style are of course the status holders in the academic world – the professors and academics who are the examiners, the editors and the referees of theses, books, articles, etc. We find a similar sort of situation with the 'house' style of a periodical. (In the more commercial world of magazines[19] the house style might well have a financial function.) Because of the power base, in this case academic power, it is possible for the question, 'Is it in the proper style' (i.e., our view of the reified academic style), to be as important as asking if the work is clearly communicating the ideas of the writer.

I am, of course, talking about secondary socialisation. The child who has grown up in an authoritarian family now moves into a democratic school situation and has to learn a whole new set of social relationships, together with their associated utterances. So the process goes on. As society changes and breaks up, so the language struggles to express and keep up with the changes and collapse of the society. As different cultures meet and mix, so their languages meet and mix; as societies gain or lose status, so do the languages.

Fishman points out (Fishman et al. 1966, p. 394) that in the United States there are prestige languages – the old Colonial languages French, Spanish and German – and the low-prestige immigrant languages – Yiddish, Hungarian and Ukrainian, for example. It is also argued that

19. There is in the two words 'periodical' and 'magazine' a social and a status value judgment. From a printing point of view they are very similar, but their markets and intentions are different. However, it is not really the thing to talk about 'magazines' in a university library committee. The sixth former often uses the two words interchangeably. The man-in-the-street is not aware of any difference – periodicals and magazines are the same.

'language maintenance in the U.S. is currently strongest amongst those immigrants who have maintained the greatest psychological, social and cultural distance from the institutions, processes and values of American core society' (Fishman et al. 1966, p. 396). Once in conflict, often the high status takes precedence and power. This sort of dominance has other language consequences. Ervin-Tripp (in Alatis 1970, pp. 311 ff.) draws attention to experiments in which Canadian Anglophones learnt French in two years in kindergarten. It is suggested that the high standard attained, as opposed to the low standard of Chicanos in the U.S., is due to the social equivalence of French with English.

'In the Montreal environment, English speaking children have no sense of inferiority or disadvantage in the school. Their teachers do not have low expectations for their achievements; their social group has power in the community; their language is respected, is learnt by Francophones and becomes the medium of instruction later in the schools. In the classroom the children are not expected to compete with native speakers of French in a milieu which both expects and blames them for their failures, and never provides an opportunity for them to excel in their own language'. This latter situation is that facing the Chicanos, and, of course, immigrants in the U.K.

Gumperz (in Alatis, 1970, p. 130) makes a similar point about the language of low-income populations in America. The evidence is that these groups have their own language structure complete and well developed, rather than a degenerate and structurally undeveloped form of the language of the accepted English norm. We have here a case of a status-superior group whose own language was status superior and thus became 'right', 'normal', etc.

He goes on to make a point of significance for social grammarians. Language choice, he suggests, is not necessarily code switching at phonological and syntax levels, but there are rules to be derived from social circumstances. One strategy uses 'foregrounding', i.e., nouns are not just names for things but also carry a host of culture-specific connotations, and it is these that are used. Thus in interlanguage discussion, this is used to include 'we' and exclude 'they'. 'This underlying meaning is then reinterpreted in the light of co-occurring contextual factors to indicate such things as degree of involvement . . ., anger . . ., emphasis . . ., change in focus . . .' (Gumperz in Alatis 1970, p. 130).

In the work done in America, there is always the emphasis on the social context. In Williams (1970) a number of authors discuss the problem of deprived, or inner-city, or educational-priority-area children. Cazden (cited by Williams 1970, pp. 81 ff.) suggests that the less-language and the different-language views of child language are inade-

quate and that we need to examine the social context. Williams himself
(1970, pp. 380 ff.) states 'that our speech by offering a rich variety of
social and ethnic correlates, each of which has attitudinal correlates in
our own and our listeners' behaviour, is one means by which we remind
ourselves and others of social and ethnic boundaries and is thus a part of
the process of social maintenance (or change)'.

One of the correlates is status at the various levels we have been
discussing. The social grammarian has to be aware not only of the
status of any group of speakers but the status of their language or sub-
languages. Conversely, by observing the language behaviour of people
in their own subcultural situation and in a multi-subculture situation,
he ought to be able to derive the status relationship of the language or
dialects of creoles.

SOLIDARITY

The second universal, I suggest, is that of friendship. This, like status, is
not an absolute but a continuum on which we can discern a number of
points. We have the stage of neutrality, the staple of much everyday
conversation, in which we are dealing with those who are, at that
moment in time, our status equals and with whom we have no emotional
reaction. From here we have various degrees of friendship indicated by
vocabulary items such as 'intimate friends', 'close friends', 'acquaint-
ances', 'casual friends'. It is essentially an informal, as opposed to a
formal, relationship capable of modification and change at the decision
of either party (or parties) involved. It is essentially a personal and
emotional link involving individuals and groups. Whilst friendship does
suggest an 'in-group' situation, the converse is not true in usual
psychology terms. Whilst two friends develop a language which has a
large element of 'shorthand' in it, it is not to be confused with jargon,
nor is it necessarily used to preserve a group identity or to reject others.
The more intimate the relationship, the fewer people involved, then the
more 'private' the communication process. What demands complete
utterances in a wider context can be reduced to words or even looks and
gestures.

In the close, emotional situation suggested by the following dialogue,
the 'involved' observer may see this as a joke or be sympathetic.

'Darling'.
'Yes darling?'
'Nothing darling; just "darling" darling',
'Darling.'

The observer from another culture may find this completely unintelligible, as has happened when I have played a recording to persons unfamiliar with the concept of romantic love between the sexes or who do not have this type of linguistic communication in their culture.

The solidarity relationship modifies the status relationship. Once again this is most easily seen in the formal institutionalized circumstances of the army. The major and the captain have a certain relationship on parade but a different one off parade where a friendship might grow up which modifies the language patterns for the inferior, who is now in a freer situation. He has more alternatives available; instead of having to circumlocute in order not to offend against the status requirements:

'I regret, sir, that I have to suggest that, perhaps you're not absolutely correct',

he is able to say

'I'm sorry, Ted, you're quite wrong'.

Just how far it is possible to go is a matter of fine subcultural judgment. Whether

'Ted, you're wrong'

will be acceptable, rather than incurring the rebuke

'Don't presume' or 'That's enough',

depends partially upon the degree of status separation; partially how near the top, or the bottom, of the status tree the participants are; whether they belong to subgroups; how authoritarian or latitudinarian the subculture is; how far the participants have freed themselves from the constraints imposed by their social status. Let us stay with the army for illustrations, but they can be duplicated in many areas of English society. It is easier for the major and the captain to have and maintain friendship than the colonel and the sub-lieutenant; a field-marshall and a general are, as it were, in such a rarefied atmosphere that they can ignore status requirements, as can the lance-corporal and the corporal, because they are so lowly in the hierachy. It is easier to have a friendship within the officer subgroup and within the N.C.O. subgroup than between the officer subgroup and the N.C.O. subgroup. In times past, these reflected real social groupings outside the army. In the rigid structure of English society, friendship could, and did, modify status in the utterance situation, but the power was always with the superior to make an end in a conversation by:

'You're going too far',
'Don't presume on our friendship'.

The involved observer, of course, can follow all these patterns and make his own value judgments about what is going on. He can subscribe to the friendship across a status gap or condemn it:

'It's good to see that Major Blank has befriended Lieutenant Blink'.
'Bad for discipline that sort of friendship; no good will come of it'.

Our social grammarian will be trying to plot the language items that make these judgments possible and, as ever, will be, by applying what he has discovered, trying to prophesy behaviour in other circumstances.

My main concern with solidarity is as a modifier of status, which I consider a much more fruitful concept at very many levels of language and at various levels of society. Solidarity has, in my present state of development, very much to do with interpersonal relationships.

However, friendship is an important universal in the social situation and whilst, so often, status determines who can be friendly with whom, human nature, or the 'cussedness of the individual', overrules, and friendship reduces language barriers and makes for a much freer conversational situation. From the 'involved' observer's point of view, when the non-linguistic signals (such as a uniform or seating or physical posture) are absent, it is often difficult or even impossible to determine status from overhearing utterances, until considerable time has elapsed. There is also the other condition, that because of friendship, two people deliberately avoid areas that would positively involve status considerations in their conversations. Finally, we have the situation in which the friendship is so close that status becomes irrelevant, and, whatever social determinants may suggest, the individual friendship determines the communication pattern so that our 'involved' observer would not be able to deduce any status relationship.

EMOTION

Emotions have had limited discussion in sociological circles. Emotions are difficult to define as they seem to involve physiological actions as well as social situations. For my purpose at the moment, I can manage with the everyday language words – anger, hate, sorrow, love (both *erotica* and *agape*), patience, impatience, surprise, etc. – those items defined and named by long and common usage in English society. They occur in interpersonal situations and once again our 'involved' observer can discern states of mind and emotional reaction:

'Cor, they aint half angry.'
'The old man'll chew his balls off.'
'If she goes on like that her Mum'll lose her temper.'

As far as language is concerned there are three appearances of emotion; three ways in which, for a social grammarian, they can affect language.
1. Neutral. This is the absence of emotion. It would include many social interactions – conventional thanks, conventional politeness – and takes in the areas where emotions do not affect language performance.
2. Joining emotions.
3. Rejecting emotions.

These last two describe the social action of the emotion and not the emotion itself. Emotions are often classified as pleasant or unpleasant; this is not my meaning here; I am concerned whether the expression of any emotion unites or separates people. Any emotion, whether unpleasant or pleasant, can join or reject. I might be angry with you, and my anger separates us; John observes my anger and agrees with it, then the anger which separates you and me joins John and me. You are sorrowing; I am sympathetic to your sorrow and so your sorrow joins us; however, Martin thinks you are daft for being sorrowful, so your sorrow separates you. Now it is important to realize that these differences are in the communication process. Logically they have to be or else all would be confusion. Sometimes the direction of the anger is made manifest:

'I'm furious with David.'

At other times it is situational. My wife comes in from shopping and slams down the basket:

'I'm furious.'

I know it isn't me, but someone or something outside. Her anger is not item-specific, but it is certainly not aimed at me. How do I know; what items of the communication process tell me that it isn't me; and how do they differ from the occasion when she comes in and says the same words, but I brace myself for the storm? What has cued me that her anger is directed at me? I dodge the issue, all I want to do is to point out that fundamental nature of emotion rejecting and emotion joining.

What emotions may be used, to whom and in what circumstances is socially determined. Once again, the highly institutionalized situation of the army helps. It is improper for the inferior to be angry with the superior. The angry 'Don't do that' is not permitted to the private as a remark to his sergeant. If he makes it in deep anxiety – 'Don't do that' he might get away with it. Nor can he be impatient; nor can he show happiness at an officer's discomfort. On analysis, the rejecting emotion situation is forbidden to the inferior. This may well have a legal force, and failure to comply may well involve formal charges and punishment.

Whilst in theory the superior has the full range of rejecting emotions at his command, in fact he may well be limited. *Noblesse oblige* might require him to allow only anger caused by dereliction of duty on the part of an inferior; the 'spirit of the law' rather than the 'letter of the law' has to be obeyed – though even here the spirit of the law may well be some reified social custom; religious taboos affect his utterance of rejecting emotions; it is against the regimental traditions to laugh at inferiors; and so on. Part of social grammar is concerned with just what is theoretically available and what constraints there are, as well as being concerned with how these social reactions are communicated.

This sort of pattern repeats itself in society in general and in the sub-cultures of society. Those with high status, to a greater or lesser degree, determine what emotions may be expressed and to whom and in what form. One can see some general propositions. The greater the social distance, the more control the superior has and the less choices the inferior has; the nearer social equality, then the more equal the choices become. (Social here must be interpreted widely as I warned before. I am not just concerned with class, but with power. Inside a classless state such as the U.S.S.R. claims to be, nevertheless there are those who strongly resent a rejecting emotion and have power to take action. Similarly in the democratic American firm, the aspiring young executive is not in a free position *vis-à-vis* his hail-fellow-well-met boss.) Solidarity modifies the emotional relationship usually in the way of freeing from emotional reaction and allowing more emotional choice. It is easier to laugh at a friend who is a superior than a non-friend superior; and similarly it is easier to ignore a rejecting emotion when solidarity is great.

Now it may well be argued that a high-status person does not take action when an inferior laughs at him. This is true, but it is his choice. For example, if on a ceremonial occasion the headmaster trips and falls, then it is *his* past actions which have built up a relationship which allows a 'guffaw of laughter' or 'a subdued titter'. Both of these phrases are redolent with social meaning – the first, for example, is almost status free as it stands; the second implies covertness as a status situation. One would be more likely to use:

1. 'The officers guffawed with laughter when their comrade received the custard pie full in the face', and
2. 'The officers gave a subdued titter when the general received the custard pie full in the face'.

Here we have semantic usage conditioned by status, but we could have:

3. 'The captain guffawed when his friend the colonel received the custard pie full in the face', and
4. 'The captain guffawed when the colonel received the custard pie full in the face'.

The ubiquitous 'involved' observer might make deductions from these such as:

on (1): 'Why not, all mates together' – status equals, with or without friendship;
on (2): 'Better be careful or the general might roast the lot of them';
on (3): 'Good job, they are friends';
on (4): 'Hope the colonel didn't hear him or he's for the high jump'.

SUMMARY

So we have the general situation that status determines what utterances can be made by whom – that the greater the social distance the greater the choice of the superior and the less the choice of the inferior. This state of affairs is modified by solidarity or friendship. The closer the friendship, the more the superior gives up his dominance, and the more the choice available to the inferior.

Emotions can be classified as either joining or rejecting. Whether the emotion is pleasant (happiness) or unpleasant (anger), it can join or separate people. Once again the superior in the status relationship determines the choice, particularly that of rejecting emotions. But also with joining emotions ('Don't be impertinent; how dare you think that your sympathy is wanted'). Here again, choices available vary inversely with social distance. In all situations the superior is not necessarily a completely free agent; he is bound by social rules and customs.

I now come to the very important special case, which is an exception to all these rules. Under the drive of a strong emotion an individual can, to coin a phrase, 'forget his station in life' and break all the rules. This is, of course, recognised in discourse by such phrases as:

'He was driven beyond endurance'; 'They pushed him too far'; 'He's almost at breaking point'.

The individual, and on occasions the group, is under such pressure, very often psychological, that the rules no longer constrain him or her. As a social grammarian one is not concerned with identifying the pressures which cause this, but with identifying the communication factors that express and also allow it to be described.

Now I would like to refer to one description of comparative language usage which illustrates both Chapter 1 Part 1 and Part 2. In the 'Report of the Twenty-First Annual Round Table Meeting on Linguistics and Language Studies' Dell Hymes (1970, pp. 69ff.) argues for a sociolinguistic basis for bilingual education rather than a purely linguistic basis and suggests that the paper by Susan A. Philips (1970, pp. 77ff) illustrates this. In an earlier paper Di Pietro has partially stated my general position, though he has a more limited view:

'If a community is socially stratified and there is variability in the language of that community, then some of the variability of language must relate to stratification' (in Alatis 1970, pp. 16–17).

In the Philips paper we see an interesting example of two different stratifications showing in language situations. The situation described occurred amongst the Warm Spring Indians and seems to have arisen from a classroom conflict situation analogous to the one I describe with West Indian girls above. It was noticed that Indian children failed to participate verbally in classroom interaction, and similarly in the playground they reacted very differently from the non-Indian children. In my terms, the Indians came from a society where status is conceived differently from the non-Indian society and where consequently the status conditioned language of the non-Indians was not meaningful to the Indians. In Philips' words:

'If the Indian child fails to follow an order or to answer a question, it may not be because he doesn't understand the linguistic structure of the imperative and the interrogative, but rather because he does not share the non-Indian assumption in such contexts that use of these syntactic forms by definition implies in an automatic and immediate response form the person to whom they were addressed. For these assumptions are sociolinguistic assumptions which are not shared by the Indians' (in Alatis 1970, p. 90).

It is pointed out that in Indian society children are encouraged to be independent at an early age, to make decisions and to carry out their lives with few orders from elders. Also the children spend much time with adults, observing conversation not participating; they observe adult tasks and the conversation involved but do not participate.

So we have the situation that in the American white society we have an elaborate status speech context with a hierarchical social context, superior dominated, i.e., a vertical language situation. Leadership is attached to ascribed leadership roles. The white child is aware of both horizontal language and vertical language for many task situations, i.e., he receives orders in a status situation from a clearcut superior who utilizes the power available to insist on obedience. He also has horizontal language between himself and his contemporaries for the same situation.

The Indian child sees leadership attached to shown expertise and learns his language in a horizontal situation, i.e., he hears the adults talking as equals and is accepted as such (though with little or no contribution allowed, but he is *learning* horizontal response; there is just no vertical language situation). In this equal status situation he has, as it were, equality of language in questioning and answering. He is always in an equality situation, not an inferior/superior situation. The Indian child goes to the white organised school and is in the inferior/superior situation which is socially, and therefore linguistically, meaningless.

This report is frustrating for me because I would like to see the actual language used in these circumstances to see just what factors are present and which absent, and just how they are related.

Part 3: Social categories of grammar

> One can hardly examine the coming and going of words without at the same time considering the pressure of cultural change. But the heart of historical linguistics has been in phonology and here, as in the study of historical grammar, linguists have been extremely wary of attributing any sort of cultural explanation to the changes they have observed (R. Burling 1970, p. 3).

In the old school grammar I was told about the subject, the verb and the object of sentences. It is the grain of truth in this suggestion that I wish to develop. Information flows in society; it flows from individual to individual, individual to group, group to group, and so on. This flow has arranged itself in patterns which can be expressed in rules. In English, one of the rules has to do with word order and the relationship of the direction of flow to the verb. Word order is significant in some languages and not in others, as is well known by linguists. I suggest that as man has struggled to classify his language he has derived a form from the there and then and has clung to these descriptions. Once again I am going back to this direction of flow and attempting to make a relationship. If I give you an order, this is a flow of language from me to you requiring you to take an action; the semantic, phonemic and other components give the direction of the flow, the social context allows the conceptual, value and response meanings to be determined and feed back into the semantic and other components some of the conceptual and value meanings. If I say to David, 'David, put that book on the table', and I use an authoritative tone of voice, then the direction of flow has to be determined, i.e., from me to David – information is passing that I want David to do something. The order and forms of words suggest an action, that of moving a book. The tone of voice says that this is an order; but society has determined that this tone is an order tone, as it has of the meaning of the words, the word order, etc. But more, society gives a context in which value judgments are made. David recognises the form 'order' but does he interpret this as an order from superior to inferior or from friend to friend? His social context gives him the framework for this value judgment; it also gives him the extra information which he requires to decide how he responds to the action. Is his self-role perception the same as my perception of David's role and so forth.

In the last section I looked at the social context; in this section I am looking at the flow of language, that material to which grammatical terms are ascribed as identification and description. The identifiers now used have lost their descriptive value except as symbols. As I showed earlier, with the concept of grammatical fit this reification of grammatical terms can cause confusion. This loss of description related to the term used requires me to use upper-case letters to indicate the traditional grammatical symbol, whilst I use lower-case letters for the social intention. For example, if the general says to the corporal 'Would you mind passing me that file please?', the grammatical form is that of a QUESTION but the social intention, the social form, is a command. There is no concept in the general's mind that the corporal will not do what is commanded. He might even qualify the QUESTION by saying that it is a REQUEST but this does not relate to the underlying situation which is that of an order. There are a number of social reasons why the general uses that particular order form, but these are face-saving devices; they do not make an order into a request.

At the present exploratory stage of social grammar I see this social function of language divided as follows:[20]

1. commands,
2. requests,
3. questions,
4. refusals,
5. responses,
6. statements,
7. (abuse).

This division is not arbitrary; it arose out of my discoveries about the function of I.S. in English compared with other languages and my need for other than current grammatical terms to discuss language in the social grammar universals of status, solidarity and emotion. Part of the problem is the constant change in function of the parts of speech (to use an old-fashioned but accurate phrase) without the consequent change of terminology. So many grammatical concepts were conceived of and given social functional terms in the early days of language description because that is how they appeared to function. However, the study of language has followed its own line of development, finishing up with its own attitudes, doctrines and terminology which have become reified and self-perpetuating but perfectly valid. Society uses language as a tool, and language is also part of society's behaviour patterns and also individual behaviour patterns. The tools have been changed and developed; indeed, like any other tool, language is abused and misused. It is subject to all sorts of personal and group vagaries. But despite all this, it has some universal and eternal[21] properties; it is these that I have coarsely listed above. In the section following I relate them in a necessarily simple way. 'Necessarily' because I am at the beginning of the work, and this first division will have to be refined, or indeed re-grouped and re-named. However, it is as I see at the moment, and my terminology is closely related to function; and as I said above, I will use terms common to grammatical description.

20. These divisions do not indicate absolute watertight compartments; rather they are identifiable points on a continuum. For convenience I treat them as discret entities, but as language reflects the complex and blurred outlines of social behaviour, its own outlines and boundaries are equally blurred. It is the old situation of 100 men lined up with the tallest at one end, the shortest at the other. We can quite happily and sensibly talk about 'tall' and 'short', but it is the boundaries which cause trouble.

21. Eternal in the time sense of being recognizable and valid at all the stages of man's history so far – as for the future one does not crystal gaze but a case can be made out that the statistical odds are in favour of stability.

Diagram 1.

Social grammar (1)	Grammatical Form (2)	Status Possibility (3)	Tone of voice (I.S. pattern) (4)	Comment (5)
1. Command	a) Order	Superior	Authoritative (Order)	
	b) Request	Superior	(1) Order (2) Request	Overruled by status context Overruled by status context
	c) Question	Superior	(1) Order (2) Request (3) Question	Overruled by status context Overruled by status context (*N.B.* The refusal of the command: Socially unacceptable; without good reason sometimes permissible)
2. Request	a) Request	Equal	Request	
	b) Question	Equal	(1) Request (2) Question	Refusal is possible, but it is an individual decision not a social decision. Socially acceptable.
3. Question	Question	Inferior	*Question* (a) Hopefully (b) Neutral (c) Despairingly	Suggested possible variants As question is going upwards favourable response is entirely at the discretion of the superior. Possibility of not even being able to ask a question.

Now a comment about the list itself. Numbers (5) and (6) – 'responses' and 'statements' – are the most tentative. I suggest, at the moment, that they are a crude division of what is left after the others have been abstracted. It is confusing; these two are not discrete; a statement may well be a response. The last one – 'abuse' – is in parentheses because there are two distinct items under this head. There is actual abuse itself, where semantic terms are intended to denigrate, insult and anger a person; and there is the use of abusive, or 'bad' , language for other social purposes, which will eventually have to be covered but is not within the purview of this paper.

The discussion about 'command', 'request' and 'question' may be helped by reference to Diagram 1. Column (1) is the *Social grammar* term; column (2) the *grammatical form;* column (3) is the class of person who uses the social grammar form; column (4) refers to *'tone of voice'*, i.e., the I.S. pattern that allows the social judgment that X is giving an order, making a request, asking a question excluding the social context. Column (5) gives additional *comment*.

1. Command

A superior can give a command by using all three grammatical forms ORDER, REQUEST OR QUESTION. The form ORDER takes an authoritative tone of voice.[22] However the form *request* ('Please would you mind moving the chair') can have one of two I.S. patterns:
    (a) the pattern associated with giving an order,
    (b) the pattern associated with making a request.
The form of the words together with the appropriate I.S. pattern does not affect the social intent of the speaker as a superior. The form QUESTION can have one of three I.S. patterns – order, request, question, but as with the REQUEST form, the social situation means an order.

In the social situation only superiors have the power to give an order; indeed the language apparatus for giving orders must have been developed by superiors. It is interesting that, in English at least, the form of the ORDER, the original function form, is short and abrupt. It requires the minimum of words, grammatical construction and I.S. pattern – just enough, and no more, to give meaning. There is no need for all the circumlocution that seems to be psychologically necessary when people

---

22. At this point it is not necessary to write out the full I.S. description; any reader conversant with spoken U.K. English has enough information for full recognition. The function of I.S. in English is discussed later.

of roughly equal status meet (cf. Goffman 1967). It is obvious that I am discussing the more extreme case here, but it is historically accurate. Until quite recently there were large numbers of people in English sub-societies who were in the position of only receiving orders from their betters (sic). Of course, this has been institutionalized in the armed forces and the police. The army's system of commissioned officers, non-commissioned officers and the rest, reflects the society in which the army was developed. There well may be a battlefield requirement of instant obedience to orders and therefore a type of communication that gave the most information in the briefest and clearest form and that had the function of obedience. There is no *necessity* for this to occur outside the battle and training for battle. The descriptions of the language patterns of the armies involved in the American War of Independence are revealing of the societies in which they were formed. The highly structured English society on the one hand and the much more egalitarian society of parts of the United States, more particularly the frontier, are reflected closely in the descriptions of their linguistic behaviour away from the battlefield and the parade ground.

From a social grammar point of view, even if they utilize a QUESTION form and I.S. pattern, a superior is, in reality, giving an order. The perceived role of the utterers is an important factor for any observer. The sort of judgment that an 'involved' observer will make depends upon his evaluation of the perceived role of the person making the remark. Similarly, there can be disagreement between the issuer of an order and the recipient. Obviously the speaker may believe he has authority to give an order and the receiver believe he has not. Also a speaker may think he has authority, but may not have the *power,* so whilst he uses the ORDER form and the authoritative tone, the recipient might resist. The recipient will make comment:

'I think you're overstepping the mark.'
'Don't give me orders.'
'Who do you think you are?'
etc.

The social grammarian should be able to deduce the relative status from these remarks and also be able to prognosticate a range of choices available in similar situations.

One final point, as society changes, then language will change with it and also the *use* of the language. By a study of the comments *about* the language of the protagonists in the status situation we learn a lot about the changes in society and also the movements of the power structures. As we see what was and what is now permissible, we can see the fluctuations in the various power structures that go to make up modern complex societies. A well-developed social grammar would, through its language analysis, shed light upon imposed power structures, upon voluntary power structures and upon perceived roles in various social situations. Further studies need to be made from a social grammarian's point of view of the work done by psychiatrists on their clients' language to shed light upon status and its influence on the study of role.

2. Request

This is essentially a function between equals. A request can have a *request* form with request I.S.; it can also have a *question* form with a request or question I.S., but the social intent is a request. In this situation a refusal is possible and socially acceptable; it depends not upon position in a social structure but upon the individual decision of the respondent. This is the staple of much conversation. It is possible, through friendship, for the status situation determining COMMANDS to change into the solidarity situation under discussion. It is a point for further discussion as to whether solidarity overcoming status is a permanent condition and irreversible or whether the solidarity is determined by the status superior. There is need of further discussion here on motivation. We are also in the realm of philosophy (in the older sense of the word), dealing with freewill and determinism, the ability of the individual to resist social pressures. We forget, for many reasons, that not only do we use language for discussing these matters, but the language used, and *by whom,* is equally revealing.

A reading of contemporary documents and historical narratives of the Civil War and Interregnum in England reveal much about attitudes, as, for example, the denying of the right of the 'rude mechanics' and 'coarse, common sort of fellows' who made up the Levellers and the Fifth Monarchy men to ask questions about democracy (see, e.g. Hill 1972 and his other works in this field). Who could use what language and when and for what purpose *and* the value judgments of observers could well prove illuminating not only on behalf of social grammarians but also, conversely, by having a proper mode of analysis, the social grammarian may well help the historian.

To return from this interesting side street, the request does not necessarily occur between permanent equals. There are many social situations in which equality is often assumed in many daily social contacts and where neutrality is socially useful. However, there is always the possibility of resentment, of overstepping the boundary and of disagreement as to status conditions. The shopping situation is a fascinating corner of language to explore. Do we discern a generation difference? With the older person deploring the lack of politeness or commenting favourably on behaviour in another shop, whilst a younger person would argue that a shop assistant is no longer a servant in status inferior sense of the word but is as good as his master.

I reiterate a warning here; in England, particularly among those with a sociology background, we tend to think always of a class situation; I am concerned with status over the *whole* field of human relationships. In the teacher/pupil relationship, where both are deeply involved in a common work project, there will be a lessening of status bounds which allows a number of questions to move into the request or even order level of performance. But it must be noticed that this is a temporary situation, at the discretion of the superior. Whether solidarity is determined solely by the status superior is an area for discussion with psychologists.

3.   *Question*[23]

This is the bottom of the ladder. I have already pointed out that the possibility of asking a question lies with the superior with the power. The intermediate area of whether one can or cannot ask questions is seen in the male/female relationship in marriage:

'She/he asked timidly/apprehensively if . . .'

This is still one of the many areas for further general and detailed investigation. All I suggest at the moment is that the question has the QUESTION form, with the question I.S., and there is probably a continuum on which points such as hopefully, despairingly, vainly, can be plotted. The question is going upwards and a response, whether favourable or unfavourable, is at the discretion of the superior.

4.   *Refusals*[24]

A refusal, in the context of social grammar, means any social process that decisively inhibits the individual's possibility of expressing emo-

---

23. A case can be made out for a change of terminology between category (3) and category (2). However, I have at the moment provisionally decided upon this nomenclature, but in the light of further exploration I could see question moving up as a category under (2) request and a different name such as 'plea' being substituted.

24. Some of the following discussion was first introduced in an article in the Nottingham Linguistic Circular (Grayshon 1973, pp. 40–45).

tions and desires or of him behaving freely in personal relationships. A refusal in such a sense is, to a greater or lesser degree, a rejection of one person by another and as such may be a deeply wounding or traumatic act.

Putting it another way; when we refuse we are, or are not, sensitive to the feelings of other people. If the social situation is such that, for whatever reason, we need not consider their feelings, then there is one set of responses. If, for whatever reason, we need to consider their feelings, then these considerations will show in language.

An initial rather crude analysis of refusal can be listed like this:

REFUSAL Outright   Any occasion   } Superior
         Conditional

         Hopeful   Status-superior   }
         Wishful   permitted   } Inferior
                      occasions

All these types of refusal are possible in a status equal or a solidarity situation; but they are not necessarily permissible.

In the community at large, refusals may have their place in the hierarchies of power; those in authority may exercise their right to refuse 'from above', but may arrange the structure of society so as to limit and even prohibit the potentially subversive counter-process of refusal 'from below'. What is prohibited may be a form of action; it may equally well be a form of speech. In short, we assume that in all societies there are situations in which 'saying no' is possible (or not possible); that there are in certain ways in which it may be said; and that there are certain meanings, implicit as well as explicit, which no-saying will convey (Grayshon 1973, p.40).

In certain societies it may well be that the possibility of refusal on the part of an inferior is not even comprehensible to a superior – for example, a slave-based society. There are specific areas of our society where outright refusal is not tolerated; these are first the areas where status is institutionalized formally as in the armed forces, prisons and many schools. Secondly, there are informally 'institutionalized' areas such as the family where small children are actively (and sometimes forcibly) discouraged from refusing. The rule that the greater the status distance the less the opportunities for the inferior to refuse can be derived.

A refusal risks an unfavourable response from the superior so an inferior can only refuse when he thinks he

(a) can get away with it without reprisals,
(b) is prepared to stand the consequences,
(c) is desperate (and our observer comments that he is defiant).

This ability, or lack of ability, to refuse is apparent in the small groups in society as well as in the big power groups. In the gang situation the leader is the one who, for many reasons, commands (sic) respect. It is no easier for the nine-year-old in a gang to refuse than it is·for his father in the labour-market situation. The constraints on the inferior are very real and even fearsome to him, whatever the observer may feel, and the refusal situation is very similar to those in the army but lies not in the institutionalizing of interpersonal relationships but in their free expression in the devious ways partially explored by group dynamics. It is of relevance to a social grammarian why people refuse, but this is a secondary stage in language analysis. First we have to reproduce language rules for recognizing the status situation which allows us to make the observation:

'He daren't refuse – he'll do what Q . . . wants'.

There are many complexities to explore – the man who, because of institutional pressures, has to agree rather than refuse, but who manages by his use of language to express his disapproval and even resentment by careful use of utterance. However, this is not the place, because we need more analyses of English before we can move into subtleties of this kind.

It should be obvious that I am discussing the social process of refusal – of 'turning down, of 'rejecting' – rather than the linguistic process of NEGATION. This latter has, of course, been treated exhaustively in manuals of grammar most recently, for example, in the large grammar by Quirk et al. (1972). The position and oppositional importance of negatives in the language system is discussed in terms of 'yes/no questions', 'assertion/non-assertion', 'negative position', etc.; but the social weight of the simple word *no* is only occasionally hinted at in the discussion (7.77 p. 406) of 'persuasive imperatives' and in other places in the text (e.g., 7.88 p. 413; 8.86 p. 518; and 10.76 p. 710). Where, as in the social situation in England, the single word *'no'* is limited to only four social situations:
(a) in institutionalized situations such as the armed forces where the abrupt *no* is used by the status superior;
(b) in childhood, when the adult strictly supervises the child's experience of the socializing process, i.e., when the child is learning to mind its P's and Q's;
(c) in states of friendship or any intimacy so close that a straight and simple *no* does not have to be softened;

(d) in situations where the power of emotion transcends the constraints of status and solidarity.

Please note, at this stage in my argument, that an observer, by observation and listening, would differentiate between (a), (c) and (d) above. Indeed I suggest that over the radio, for example, just listening to the way in which *no* is said would allow a percipient listener to derive the appropriate one of these three situations. This provokes the question of how this is done, which I explore in the next section.

5. Responses

This, and the next heading, I am only just beginning to explore. In the social situation, language is a continuous initiation/response situation with feedback (both positive and negative). How any one person holds up his end of the conversation will depend upon many factors, but both at a gross and a detailed level status will affect what is said and how it is said (Goffman 1967, pp. 113ff.). The initiation of conversation, and the termination of it, is in the hands of the superior at that particular time. Only amongst those who consider themselves equal (either temporarily or permanently) is there freedom to start or finish conversation at will. Even then there are social considerations such as politeness or considerations that require particular forms of starting or finishing. Solidarity is important for release from social forms of politeness. If I want to draw attention to a minor mistake or disagreement I can use a variety of introductory remarks in an order something like this:

'Excuse me, I'm awfully sorry but I think there's something wrong here . . .'
'I say, John, there's something wrong here . . .';
'John, what's wrong here . . .?'
'John, what have you been up to . . .?'
'John, you're a clot . . .'

Note here the QUESTION form used as a statement in order to fulfil the *social* function of softening a particular approach. By asking a question one is apparently asking for help; the speaker knows what is wrong, but by asking the person who made the mistake to find it himself, the speaker is allowing him to save 'face' (Goffman 1967, pp. 113ff.). The last two imply close relationships where face is not important, and, particularly with the last one, there can be mutual amusement at each other's mistakes.

However, I have not given enough information in the printed word above for these deductions to be made; my analysis has assumed *how* these words were said. We need qualifications from the adverbs of manner (sic)

said angrily, said placatingly, said inquiringly, said accusingly, etc.

In my analysis I have assumed a joining emotion base for the utterances. Take the first of the two question forms; these can be further sub-divided according to the manner in which they have been said. We have assumed a joining emotion, so then we can have a number of possibilities:

(a) Said angrily. With the anger directed away from John and thus suggesting a third party is at fault.
(b) Said with a neutral voice. Suggesting a mistake but not laying blame anywhere.
(c) Said inquiringly. Suggesting a search for information, again without laying blame, but suggesting a greater degree of politeness than (b).
(d) Said placatingly. Showing that you know John is at fault but that you don't want to accuse him.
(e) Said diffidently. Knowing there's a mistake, but wondering:
  (1) either how important it is,
  (2) or drawing attention to the mistake, suggesting that it is some-what reprehensible, but not wanting to upset the friendship.

Social grammarians are concerned, not with listing the adverbs or classifying the adverbs which modified the verb *said* in the list above but with identifying the components of language which allow the participants and the observer to make or define these social actions. (This is the stuff of the next section.)

This whole area is full of complexities yet to be explored, and, of course, they have to be related to the placement of questions for example. It might well be that this needs a further division in the light of further study.

6. *Statements*

This should, perhaps, be put in inverted commas – I use it because it looks better than 'remnants'! I suspect that, whilst I intend this for all those items left out when the other five sections have been defined, there might be no need for it. At the moment I see it containing those comments we make to ourselves when no one else is present – the comments addressed to an inanimate object with the intention of encouraging ourselves or it; the 'thinking aloud' we all do from time to time. The whole use of language by an individual for his own purposes. Perhaps this is the beginning of a whole new field of endeavour for a psychosocial grammarian!

7. Abuse

This, once again, is a description of a social action – that of insulting. I am not talking about swearing, blasphemy or cursing, nor necessarily the words derived from these categories. First we must distinguish between being shocked and being insulted, though the first might be part of the second on occasions or be used to bring about the second; nevertheless they are different. This is best shown by illustration. If you had a very close friend who was a nun whom you regularly visited, and she greeted you one day by saying:

'Now you fat-arsed old bugger, how are you?',

you would be shocked but not necessarily insulted. The social expectation of polite, respectful 'pure' language is the norm. Vulgarities and 'dirty' words are not expected, and you are surprised and shocked, but because you were spoken to in a friendly, affectionate and welcoming way, you are not insulted. You may feel that the nun has been sinful and behaved very badly, but your personal relationship has not been attacked by the words. There is the possibility that you might make an insult where an insult is not intended. You might argue that the use of anything but the best of language used by a nun to you implies that the nun thinks of you as a person who does not have polite language standards – but here again, the insult lies not in the particular words but in misjudgment of your behaviour patterns.

Abuse may well lie in the semantic level. There are words and phrases in different cultures that imply insults; they take their function from the society in which they arise and do not travel well. I have a most unjustified reputation for saintliness in one particular area of Nigeria. In a discussion at one church meeting, tempers got out of control, and I was accused of being the bastard son of an illegitimate she-camel. This in its original language is the sort of insult that in the immediate past would have led to violence, and even now if I had walked out or retaliated with verbal action, I would have been within my social rights. Whilst knowing intellectually that this was an insult, nevertheless emotionally and socially it was at the most amusing but more probably almost meaningless. In the event, I passed it over with a look of surprise and went on as if nothing had occurred. This thoroughly disconcerted the speaker and his friends; indeed my 'loving and saintly' behaviour so upset them that they apologized, and what had been a most acrimonious meeting became a meeting of concern and cooperation. The theological implications I leave aside; the point I'm making is that the intention of insult was not carried over because of different social awareness patterns.

One area of the social origin of the terms of abuse has relevance to our main theme. Some items are drawn from a much inferior strata of society and are applied to a status equal – 'cotton picking' – as adjectival phrase. The people who picked cotton were the Negro slaves, and to call someone a 'cotton picking...' is to imply that he is no better than a slave. Then there is the utilizing of an action that is possible but rare or nonexistent. Polsky (1967, pp. 129–130) points out that in the American kinship there are three basic types of incest, brother-sister, father-daughter and mother-son, and that there is derived from the partner of one of these a term of abuse 'motherfucker'. In fact, the actual role-incumbents are rare, and enquiries made by Polsky at the Institute of Sex Research revealed that there was only one case in their records that they considered genuine. I suggest here that we have a case of the rarity of an anti-social action lending strength to a word in order to make it into an insult. But these two words of insult are revealing for my general theory because we see an example of a high status using a low-status job to create an insult, whilst the lowest status, the very bottom of the heap – the Negro slave – cannot utilise this aspect of society – it does not exist for him; so he has to search amongst socially deviant behaviour for an insult. Obviously there are other sources of abuse such as animal terminology and excreta and so forth. I am drawing attention to this one area derived from status.

Solidarity, friendship, modifies abuse by making it lose its semantic intent. A close friend can use abusive words without giving offence. Often an observer perceives close friendship by observing that two people are careless with insulting terms. During my stay in Nigeria between 1950 and 1960 I had a close Nigerian friend who often put his head in the staff room and asked if that 'imperialist bastard' was about, whilst I reciprocated with 'ignorant black bastard'. It was interesting that our close friendship allowed us to turn these terms on their head, not only in private but in semi-public amongst persons to whom these terms could have been offensive and to whom we would not have used them.

This leads me to another source of abuse; the culturally opposite – 'imperialist bastard', 'commie bastard', 'Trotskyite', etc. The Kremlin watchers and the Peking watchers are concerned to discover which is the 'outgroup' and the terms used to describe deviant behaviour, 'revision-ism', etc. When we observe the splinter left-wing groups outside the communist block, we see them using these terms to abuse one another. The involved observer may share in the pain (or pleasure) of the insult; the observer notes the fact but is not involved. However, the abuse is firmly socially based. Abuse does not always need two parties; as I showed above abuse might lie only in the mind of the abuser or the abusee. To insult can also be unintentional because of a lack of proper understanding of the social situation. Social grammar is concerned with identifying just what is insulting and in what social circumstances otherwise normal utterances become potentially insulting. There is also the necessity of considering just *where* in the features of communication the insult is carried. Not only must the social situation give information about whether insults are intended, but also the carriers of the information must give information because in English it is possible to give the absolutely opposite information to that which the semantic content would indicate. This is particularly obvious in abuse and in using negatives, and it might well be the extreme case of intention and meaning shift that has been mentioned already under the discussion of lack of grammatical fit. There is the condition of lack of semantic fit; in the relationship cited above, my semantic meaning was to suggest that my friend was illegitimate and ignorant and that both of these were socially unacceptable, but I also inferred that his pigmentation is socially undesirable. The intention, accepted by him and by involved observers, was one of friendliness. Where is the information carried? And what happens in other languages?

The converse of this can apply. Socially acceptable words and phrases can have an insulting intention and be recognized as such. This can be situational as in regular committee meetings where one speaker of my acquaintance has the habit of saying 'with due respect Mr. Chair-man . . .' and then proceeding to ruthlessly tear his opponent to pieces. He has the cue phrase 'with due respect . . .' which warns the regular members of that group of his behaviour pattern. However, it is not so much this special case that I am thinking about, but the way in which an innocuous word can be made deadly. There is a difference between 'John, you idiot' said one way and 'John, you idiot' said another. The extreme form of this is sarcasm, where the semantic intention is belied by the other information factors. It has been pointed out to me by many overseas students that sarcasm is more common in English than in other languages and that it has to do with the control of emotion. Greek students have often commented that, because they give vent to their emotions physically and semantically, obviously there is less need to be sarcastic. Sarcasm comes under the heading of abuse because it has the intention of more traditional abuse of hurting the recipient. If I may be allowed to speculate a little, I would suggest that sarcasm is the product of two main social processes in its more sophisticated form. Firstly it involves considerable language ability at various levels and requires considerable physiological and emotional restraint; secondly this restraint may well be the product of a social order that disapproves of manifest emotional displays. In eighteenth-century England in certain levels of society, to show great emotion, more particularly anger, was socially unacceptable. But one needs to show the strong disapproval which is so often a content of anger; I suggest that the irony and mild sarcasm were developed to fit this need. Now sarcasm has become a very definite weapon in the language armoury; so much so that one can court social disapproval by using it on unsuitable antagonists, viz. the advice often given to new teachers not to use sarcasm with younger children as they are defenseless.

CONCLUDING REMARKS

In this part I have been concerned with the division of language by intention in the social situation. 'Prescriptive' grammars have utilized social terms at the semantic level, and at the level of word order. But as meanings of words and functions of word order have changed and developed under complex social pressures, the 'prescriptive' grammar terms have been severed from their original relationship. This, just because they were concerned with form at a particular point in time. I am seeking a description which will allow the recognition of social pressures but also the ability of the individual to operate language, not only as a social action but as his own particular weapon and tool in the cultural situation. We then have to recognize that when we ask a question we are approaching someone else, and we are concerned with his appreciation of our intention. A question is potentially a disturbing thing; it could be a weapon which upsets our self-control and our self-evaluation or cause us to lose face. The questioner must signal his intention of *not* doing this, and the social grammarian is concerned with defining those parts of the communication process which enable not only the 'surface' information but the personal and social intention of the speaker and relate these to what is socially permissible. By using the concept of question intention rather than question form, and by setting this in the relationships superior/inferior, solidarity, joining and rejecting emotion rather than forms such as class, ingroup/outgroup, etc., the social grammarian has some chance of producing a description which will allow for cross-cultural difference and change and development in societies and sub-societies.

As Lapiere has said in the purely sociological context:

Even now, in the midst of the most rapid social change that man has ever experienced, the social *ideal* would seem to lean towards the glorification of stability and the depreciation of change, as witness the fact that most contemporary sociological writing is concerned with structure rather than process, with the state of things as they are rather than with how they came to be that way and in what directions they are going (1965, p.2).

If we substitute 'language' for 'social' and 'sociological' we have a comment on much linguistic work. A social grammarian must be concerned how things happened, why they are and where they are going.

As is reasonable, this study relies upon sociological and social-anthropological insights – after all it has to do with language in society; but in all this the individual must not be lost sight of. When I talk about status determining, I definitely do *not* mean blind forces, nor do I wish to subscribe to evolutionary theory either Comptian or Marxist, or Gemeinschaft-Gesellschaft; nor do I subscribe to either Utopian or Spenglerian views. Change, yes, but not a hidden moral evaluation of change. I *do* place importance on the function and choice of the individual in the cultural process. I agree with Lapiere's thesis that the changes that occur within a society are social, that a change in society comes not through an organic process, but through a violation of the normal process.

'A change in society comes, even as does a tumour in an organism, as a foreign unwanted agent, not necessarily of destruction, but always of disturbance to the established and organizationally preferred structures and processes of life' (Lapiere 1965, p. 39).

Thus the individual is important in language. He uses it for his own purposes; if he is an inferior it is the individual that challenges the superior through the use of language (see page 65). It is the inferior with knowledge and ability who challenges the superior and seeks to control and reduce the superior's power. Language is behaviour; it can also be power maintenance structure. It is socially conditioned but individually handled. Shakespeare was part of his society, but he was an individual and it is *his unique use* of his language in a social setting that we cherish. This paragraph is a reminder that any language group is made up of individuals using language; if one of them can use language a little differently, a little more efficiently, then he can use his language superiority to counter others' superiority in another facet of life. And here is one of the greatest complications for any student of language – he is using his subject to discuss and evaluate itself. As he goes through the very process of model making that I am attempting, he inevitably moves away from language towards alienation and reification. This is at his stage of scholarship, I suggest, inevitable, but we ought to acknowledge that we *are* doing it, and be aware of the consequences.

CHAPTER III

Social Information Carriers

'Equivalence in difference is the cardinal problem of language and the pivotal concern of
linguists. . .' (R. Jakobson 1966, p. 233).

In this chapter I make a beginning at finding out where social information lies in English, more particularly in the non-semantic features, and
comparing this – in a very limited way – to three Nigerian languages. I
am most definitely not attempting even a partial analysis and comparison of English with these languages. At the most I am saying 'Here are
some features in language not noticed before; they are suggestive of
further avenues to explore not only for a social grammar but for
language more generally'. I suggest here and now that one of the
functions of social grammarians is to push on with the analysis I
tentatively begin in this section and make a fund of new insights into
language available for others who approach language differently. I
dearly long to investigate further and in much more depth, but facilities
and time are not yet available as far as I am concerned; but I do believe
that there is enough information here in this preliminary investigation
for me to have made out a case for work to be done.

My thoughts were started off by two very different pieces of work.
Whilst preparing some lectures on the concept of role, I came across an
unpublished thesis by Abravanel (1962). He writes up an experiment
where two sets of subjects both listened to one end of a telephone
conversation. However they were given different information about the
speaker and the listener involved in the conversation. The two groups
made different value judgments about the behaviour of the speaker
according to their interpretation of his role. The other is the recording
'John and Marsha' by the comedian Stan Freberg in which he uses only
the two names John and Marsha to tell the tale of seduction. He uses
carefully chosen, soft, sweet music to reinforce the voices. To pass his
information he uses the I.S. pattern in the voices. I sometimes use this to

illustrate one of the functions of intonation and stress in English. However, I was struck by the fact that just occasionally some overseas students found it incomprehensible. They fell into two groups – those who apparently did not have this verbal emotional relationship in their culture, and those whose mother tongues were tonal language (by chance they came from West Africa) and who, whilst competent in vocabulary and grammar, were unable to cope with our I.S. pattern.

Now in the case of both Abravanel and Freberg, they relied upon the listener's (observer's) appreciation of the social context of the utterances to give meaning to the words and sentences. And equally important from the Abravanel study, – the value judgments, that one person was rude and the other not rude, were related not so much to the words or the tone of voice but to the social relationships implied by these linguistic phenomena.

The fact of I.S. features being related to emotion is well known, and the English language is full of phrases illustrating this. It is interesting that most of these phrases are for written work. This is particularly true of adverbs of manner attached to verbs describing speech action. At the crude stylistic level:

'He said angrily . . .'
'He laughingly said . . .'
'With misery in his voice he replied . . .'
'Her voice bubbled with happiness as she replied . . .'

and so on. In normal conversation we use this form but rarely; we conduct our conversation directly quoting the person:

'Well, I said to him . . .'
'And he said to me . . .'
'And I said . . .'
and so on.

I go so far as to say that the whole apparatus of changing into indirect speech (and to a lesser degree the reverse) is a literary device to reduce boredom in reading and to make for a smoother, 'better' style. This was pointed out by Church, who says:

Written utterances, of course, must be made more elaborate than the spoken ones, to compensate for the lack of concrete common context and the nonverbal props – gestures, expressions, intonations – available to the speaker (1961, p. 125).

Of these nonverbal props, Birdwhistell (1970), Lamb (1965) and Scheflen (1972) already referred to, have looked at gestures and expressions; I am concerned with the intonations, indeed with that group of paralinguistic features for which I use the symbol I.S.

Now these patterns have been exhaustively examined (Crystal 1969), but the fundamental difference from my approach is that all these analyses are concerned with form. Whilst recognizing that I.S. in one or more of its features has relevance to meaning, social conditions, etc., they have not been able to give a related classification. In the current work amongst sociolinguists the importance of these features is noticed, and correlations have been made between various items and social class, for example. But the analysis is limited by the basic analysis of I.S. features in current linguistic theory.

CONTRADICTION OF MEANING

The first and most important point I want to make is that I.S. normally works alongside the item 'word' and the item 'syntax', i.e., it supports semantic and grammatical meaning, but when the signal sent by the word and syntax contradicts the signal sent by I.S., then I.S. has priority. This, of course, lies embedded in the social context which determines according to status and solidarity just who may *say* what and to whom.[25]

The easiest area to see this is in language. My very unlikely nun (above page 87) is not insulting but giving a very friendly greeting. Crude sarcasm is obviously another area. Indeed in English I suggest that normally the insult is carried rather in the I.S. than in the word or word order.

'I don't think that was very sensible'

can have a far more devastating effect when said in a particular way, than any collection of swear words.

The most common area of change of meaning is in the inflexion of a question:

'You're coming home?'

By changing the I.S. this statement becomes a question. By changing I.S. this question/statement becomes an order or a plea. Functionally

---

25. There is a most interesting area to explore as to how far the inferior can get away with communicating disagreement: for example, by using respectful semantic form but utilising I.S. but not sarcasm or irony – the next stage on from dumb insolence, no longer a crime in the army; it is a device often used in situation comedy.

there is a tremendous difference between these intentions and response to them in a social intercourse. They are without doubt part of the meaning.

This can lead to problems in interlanguage communion. When teaching in Nigeria I found it most dangerous to use the word 'nonsense' to students, even of mature years. It provoked sorrow, resentment, sulking, even covert hostility. I found it impossible to soften it in any way by utilizing I.S., even to the extent of joking. As I have since discussed, the different function of I.S. prevented its English communication function of turning semantic abuse into friendliness, from being perceived – though there is the possibility of a role conflict which allows the superior to make a joke in English society but not in other societies.

There is a further function of I.S. which is to provide a communication feature for social roles that have left the semantic realm. To my mind the most outstanding case is that of the second person singular 'thou' in English. This usage has just vanished, except in certain dialect situations. This is often contrasted with the French 'tu' and the distinction this allows between the formal and the familiar. But, if the participants wish, and sometimes when they try to conceal it, observers can judge the intimacy of speakers by listening to how they say things. The intimate relationship of brother and sister, or close friends, is easily identifiable in English; it lies in the I.S. patterns. It might be correct to say that English lacks the second person singular personal pronoun, but it is incorrect to say that we are unable to express this relationship in English. The situation of number, whether I am talking to one or more than one, i.e., singular v. plural, is somewhat different; but even here it is often possible to distinguish the single recipient of the remark from the collective group to whom it is addressed (Lieberman 1967, McIntosh and Halliday 1966, Trager 1958, pp. 1–12, Trager and Smith 1951, Chomsky and Halle 1968).

SOCIAL FUNCTION OF I.S.

I.S. gives the clue for role differentiation and for the judging of roles. Whether a person was rude or impertinent in Abravanel's study was an appreciation of patterns of utterances in social situations: what was and was not permissible to certain groups in society. But this lies in the I.S. as well as in words, and in many situations it lies in the I.S. *rather than* in words. Allied with this is the use of words and I.S. to suggest a general social mode.

Taking the latter point first – the use of words and I.S. to suggest a general social mode: I have recorded whole days of BBC news broadcasts; there is careful choice of words such as a 'male child' instead of 'boy' and 'received fatal injuries' instead of 'was killed', and all is said on a careful level dispassionate tone. The whole intention is to reduce emotional tension, to be rational and level-headed about what is an emotional and upsetting occurrence. There is a tradition largely unarticulated that if there is emotion then it cannot be rational, and this is part of the success of the older tradition in BBC news broadcasts. The disembodied voice speaking in a level unemotional voice was almost a guarantee of objectivity.

I have pointed out above that the status superior has control of what can be said, but the status superior also has the decision as to what is rude, impertinent, cheeky – all social judgments upon someone else's behaviour patterns. Therefore what is cheeky or rude in language is also a social judgment. However, in the male/female relationship, for example, the words giving this judgment are often contradicted by the I.S.:

(a) 'Let's sneak away from the party and go to my place';
(b) 'What a suggestion'.

(a) is made by the male of the species; (b) is made by the female, and the words imply a rebuke; the I.S. pattern can well be an encouragement. A little later on one person makes a suggestion and the other replies:

'What sort of girl do you think I am?'

Again, a rebuke – apparently – but with the appropriate I.S. pattern, it could be an invitation to carry on. A little later on is heard the words:

'Darling, don't'

But if darling didn't then he would have been guilty of complete misunderstanding! The words say 'no' – the I.S. says 'carry on' (Grayshon 1973).

In the teacher/child situation there can be differing functions of the words and the I.S.; there is the need to rebuke and correct the child but at the same time to reassure. A most careful and necessary attempt to separate the sin from the sinner. The words tell of the sin; the I.S. reassures the child of the continual and continuous care of the teacher. As a frequent visitor I have noticed that in infant schools the teachers tend to exaggerate the I.S. pattern and to use I.S. far more than is common in later life. With the reception class in its early days this is particularly noticeable and is reinforced with gestures and actions. On discussing this with teachers they first say that they are unaware of the practice and secondly say that they need to reassure the children; some, having thought a little more deeply about the function of language, suggest that children respond to the tone of the voice as much as to the words, and that some of the children come into school with very limited language ability as regards language and grammar.

THE EMOTIONAL FUNCTION OF I.S.

It has long been recognized that I.S. has to do with emotion, but there has been little success in devising rules. It is obvious from the range of adverbs of manner dealing with emotion that can be attached to verbs showing language behaviour that there must be a pattern:

He . . . said
    . . . replied
    . . . commented
    . . . asked
    . . . demanded
    . . . etc.

    . . . kindly
    . . . angrily
    . . . impatiently
    . . . with surprise
    . . . lovingly
    . . . caringly
    . . . furiously
    . . . etc.

How do I make these interpretations? How as an observer am I able to write to a third party that Joe was furious when he told us about the action or when I actually tell someone this and reenact the situation saying the words in the way that Joe said them? The information must lie in the I.S. pattern because I make different judgments on the same sentence semantically and grammatically speaking.

As a first attempt at an analysis[26] I took just one type of question usually referred to as a rhetorical question and looked at the function of I.S. and its relation to grammar and the speaker's intention and emotional state. A rhetorical question is of the form to be outlined, but

26. The first part of the argument that follows – to do with the comparison between Yoruba and English – appeared originally in an article in *Language and Society* (Grayshon 1975a).

it is a particular case where the *social* expectation is that no one will necessarily answer. The question form can be used to require an answer from a third person. The form, then, is of the variety:

'Is B going to Q Y'

where B is a person, named or classified, Q is a verb form, and Y is a pronominal component. The actual example I use is:

'Is Margaret going to wear that hat?'.

Trying this sentence I analysed it in the following way. Using the chart (Fig.1) I took each word in the sentence in turn and held the stress constant and changed the intonation pattern; at the same time the remainder of the sentence was kept constant. On the chart

Column (1) is the identifying number.

Column (2) is the word under consideration.

Column (3) is the rise and range of the voice on the emphasized word in column 2.

The scale used is a five-point scale similar to the tonic, mediant, dominant, seventh, tonic, scale in Western music and which can be shown diagrammatically like this:

d tonic		high
c dominant 7th		
b dominant		
a mediant		
a- tonic		low

with *a* the normal speech level as the mediant, and the voice rising as we move up the stave. It is most difficult to hold to *a* and increase emphasis, so it rarely occurs. The fall *a* to *a-* at the end of a sentence is the equivalent in music to a plagual cadence or a perfect cadence.

Column (4) is the level of stress or, in social terms, emphasis level. This is also graded on a five point scale: *d* very strong, *c* strong, *b* strongish, *a* normal, *a-* soft.

Column (5) describes the voice level over the rest of the sentence with the final word given any movement where relevant.

Column (6) indicates the emotion involved in the utterance.

Column (7) shows general remarks.

The following signs indicate movement of the voice:

↘ fall over word (or words).
↗ rise over a word.
↗↘ last word or last two words form a perfect cadence.

Figure 1.

	Word	Rise	Emphasis level	Movement in rest of sentence	Emotion	Remarks
(1)	(2)	(3)	(4)	(5)	(6)	(7)
1	is	b	a	a hat		Straightforward request
2	is	c	b	a hat	Impatience	Usually specific 3rd party being addressed
3	is	c	c	a hat	Very impatient	Ditto
4	is	d	d	a hat	Extreme imp.	Limit of patience Usually specific 3rd party being addressed
5	Margaret	b	a	a hat		Straightforward request
6	Margaret	b ↘	b	a hat		Straightforward request
7	Margaret	b ↗	a	a hat		Straightforward request
8	Margaret	b ↘	b	a hat	Anger	Particular addressee or rhetorical
9	Margaret	c ↘	c	a hat	More anger	Particular addressee or rhetorical
10	Margaret	d ↘	d	a hat	Very angry	Particular addressee or rhetorical
11	going	b	a	a hat		Straightforward request unlikely, difficult to say
12	going	b ↘	a	a hat		Difficult to say
13	going	c ↘	b	a hat		Unlikely; not usual
14	going	d ↘	c	a hat		Unlikely; not usual
15	to	n.a.				Always unaccented; last syllable of verb
16	wear	b ↘	a	a hat		Straightforward request
17	wear	c ↘	b	a hat		Unlikely; not usual

Figure 1. (Continued)

Word	Rise	Emphasis level	Movement in rest of sentence	Emotion	Remarks
(1)	(2)	(3)	(4)	(5)	(6)	(7)

(1)	(2)	(3)	(4)	(5)	(6)	(7)
18	wear	d ⬎ c		a hat		Unlikely; not usual
19	that	a ⬎ a		a hat		Straightforward request
20	that	b	b	a hat		Indicating a particular hat
21	that	c	c	a hat	Incredulity	Indicating a particular hat
22	that	d	d	a hat	Incredulity	Indicating a particular hat
23	hat	a ⬊ a		a hat		Straightforward request
24	hat	b ⬊ b		a hat		Straightforward request
25	hat	b ⬊ c		a hat		Rare
26	hat	-a ⬈ a		a hat		Straightforward request
27	hat	b	a˙	a hat		Straightforward request
28	hat	c	a	a hat		Rare. Emphasis level
29	hat	d	a	a hat		doesn't affect, so no
30	hat	ba ⬈ a		a hat		point in including
31	hat	abc ⬈ a		a hat		

The first step was to fill in the form for situation one, as shown in Figure 1. I listed the words in order down the sentence then, taking each word in turn, and holding the rest of the sentence constant, I varied the pitch of the voice showing the change by letter and symbol. It quickly became evident that – as was apparent in other work – emphasis and pitch go hand in hand, though sometimes stress lagged behind (*cf.* item 2). My next intention was to hold the first word in the sentence in a stressed position and move the other words whilst holding the rest of the sentence to a similar pattern. After that, the first two words would have been held at a high pitch and the remainder varied and the rest of the sentence held – and so on through the possible permutations. However, and very fortunately, I decided to do an initial analysis of the first situation (Fig.1). Immediately a pattern stood out. Numbers 2, 3 and 4 revealed impatience; items 8, 9 and 10 showed anger; items 21 and 22 showed incredulity: in each case, the greater the pitch and the stronger the emphasis, the greater the emotion involved. Out of the 31 patterns possible for this sentence, eight concerned emotions, 23 were possible variants for a straightforward question. Two points must be made here: first 'possible' in the sense that they could be conceivably used by a native speaker of English, but items 5, 11, 12, 13, 14, 17 and 18 are rarely used, possibly because they are difficult to say; item 15 is so unnatural because we try to emphasize a preposition (which in this case is part of the verb and is in fact a last unaccented syllable of the verb). So we are left with the situation that a native English speaker has a possible thirteen ways of asking this question in a straightforward unemotional manner. It must not be thought that each of the steps in the analysis is separate from the next step. They are points identified on a continuum, and where one begins and another ends is difficult, if not impossible, to determine. (This is often the cause of misunderstanding in verbal communication: a group of people who frequently converse can be aware of quite subtle differences; others not so familiar may well misunderstand and make untoward value judgments based on their own personal relative experience of utterances in a different small subculture.) In my original analysis I worked through 32 possible variations and from these identified the three emotions under discussion. By sampling first the emotion carrying I.S. patterns and then a selected sample of others, I checked out the many remaining possible variations. The emotions which showed up were all unpleasant or rejecting emotions; they were:

(a) anger, occurring in items 8, 9 and 10;
(b) impatience, occurring in items 2, 3 and 4;
(c) incredulity, occurring in items 21 and 22.

The analysis shows that a similar I.S. pattern is used in each of these cases. It is the combination of these patterns with grammatical features, the whole located in a cultural context, which has produced this form of information transfer.

Let us look at these emotions more carefully; we can see certain social implications: the first one, anger, is caused by a person (in this case Margaret): in older grammatical terms, the subject of the sentence; in behavioural terms, the trigger for the emotion. If we had a sentence such as:

'Is this *bloody engine* going to work?'

the 'bloody engine' is the trigger for the emotion. This is the initiator of the emotion in the speaker. Functioning in the utterance it always appears after the auxiliary verb, that part of the verb which starts the question form. Anger is a physiological process. When we express it there are body changes of many kinds – clenched fists, raised eyebrows or frowning eyebrows, etc. As far as utterances are concerned there are three physiological changes of the vocal machinery: the throat is constricted; the voice is raised in volume; and the voice is raised in pitch.[27] Elsewhere I would like to discuss the effect of social training which frowns upon manifesting these emotionally triggered physiological features; space precludes it here.

From the foregoing we see that the I.S. features fall on the nominal of the question and that we have an emotion triggered by the nominal actor in the utterance.

From a careful look at impatience we see that this is caused by what the nominal is actually doing; the I.S. is on the verbal component. It is the 'wearing' action that causes the emotional upset. The I.S. can be either on the auxiliary verb or on the main verb or on both. These, to the more discriminating listener, may indicate degrees of impatience. I suggest, then, that impatience is expressed by similar physiological features as in anger, but then they are transferred to the verbal component. Impatience is an emotion triggered by an *action* of the nominal in the sentence and produced in the speaker.

Finally we examine surprise or incredulity. The speaker is surprised by the pronominal component, the object of the verb. The I.S. is on the pronominal component, the object of the verb. The I.S. is on the pronominal of the predicate of the sentence, to once again use oldfashioned terms. The emotion is caused by the understanding of the listener of this predicate part of the sentence. The speaker is concerned with the totality of action – the wearing of a hat. In English surprise has been attached to the pronominal part of this action – the hat. We now come to one of the subtleties of the English language. Suppose I need to express surprise and I have no pronominal? Then the I.S. pattern changes on the nominal and the verbal components; we have a double rise fall:

'Is that engine going to work?'

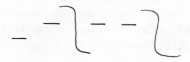

27. In all the discussion that follows it is obvious that the material needs to be reworked with the aid of a fully trained phonetician to cope with the subtleties of the expressions of the human voice.

Here again, as much as I would like to explore further, space forbids. There is a further complication with regard to incredulity. The speaker of the utterance may be surprised about the hat that Mary is going to wear, and therefore we have the pattern I suggest occurring on the pronominal; but suppose the utterer is surprised that Mary is going to be the wearer rather than Edna or Jean? We would then logically expect the I.S. pattern to move from the pronominal to the nominal. But we have already used this pattern for anger; therefore an alternative pattern is used; it is rather subtle, there is the drop from high to low, but the low position is much stronger and is more voiced than in anger.

Margaret

Anger, I remind you, is a single high pitch. There can be a physiological difference which is related to throat position due to the increase of muscular tension in anger whilst incredulity comes in a more nasal way. However I do not wish to examine or analyse this difference in detail because the throat action is not a necessary condition of the difference between anger and incredulity.

Anger:	Rise in pitch, strong emphasis on the first syllable with the second and subsequent symbols being 'thrown away' and a small fall on the second syllable. These I.S. features occur on the nominal.
Impatience:	Rise in pitch and emphasis; no fall. I.S. features occur on the auxiliary verb.
Incredulity: (a)	Rise in pitch, strong emphasis, rise held across all syllables until the last. (Similar to anger.) I.S. features occur on the pronominal.
(b)	Rise in pitch, strong emphasis but the fall is on the last syllable of the word (or words) but with more emphasis than in anger so that this syllable is not thrown away. I.S. features occur on the nominal.

The time has come when I can postulate a number of laws:

1. The information clues to emotions in an utterance of questions are based on definite I.S. patterns which are related to definite grammatical features. Word meaning, semantic arrangements and cultural demands may modify and/or increase choice, but the basic communication factor is I.S.

2. (a) When anger is intended, then the I.S. pattern falls on the nominal, i.e., to the person, thing or idea at which the anger is directed.

(b) When impatience is intended, then the I.S. falls on the verbal component, i.e., impatience is associated with action (in the wider sense of the word).

(c) When surprise or incredulity is intended then the I.S. falls on, either:

(1) the pronominal component when the surprise is concerned with behaviour directed at that component; or

(2) the verbal component where there is no pronominal; or

(3) the nominal where exasperation is with the initiator of the behaviour expressed in the utterance.

3. The same I.S. pattern is possible on the particular nominal and the verbal, the difference in emotional meaning is related to the grammatical component. With regard to the expression of impatience then there is a difference in I.S.

4. The I.S. patterns for the emotions cited and their grammatical relations are:

Anger	High-low	Strong emphasis on high	Placed on nominal
Impatience	High	Strong emphasis	Placed on initial verbal component
Incredulity	(a) High-low	Strong emphasis	Placed on pronominal
	(b) High-low	Emphasis on both	Placed on main verb
	(c) Double High-low	Strong emphasis	Placed on nominal

5. Intensity of emotion varies directly with rise in pitch, increase of stress, increasing loudness of voice and, where relevant, increase of intonation jump. These increases may often be related to comparative adjective/adverb sequences, but vocabulary change is more related to alternance, cultural background and cultural intention. These laws are fixed and allow of no variation in the English situation as it stands at the moment. The expression of emotion must be common to a language group; otherwise communication is not possible. However, there are other features which may be joined to these. For example, the increases in intensity of I.S. to give a stronger emotion may be related to comparative adjective/adverb/noun sequences.

'Is Margaret going to wear that hat?'
can become
'Is Margaret going to wear that bloody hat?'

Our observance of the utterance as a third party may allow us to describe the emotion in a variety of terms, e.g.,

(a) John was surprised that Mary was going to wear that hat;
(b) John was incredulous when Mary said that she was going to wear that hat.

In written rather than spoken language we may report the utterer as

'speaking through clenched teeth', or
'Speaking with quiet, cold, deadly intent'.

But as a general rule vocabulary change and grammatical change are related more to matters of choice, cultural background or cultural intent.

When we go on to examine the range of question forms it would be logical, and also make cultural sense, if the rules derived from the examination of one question form were common to all question forms. As I hope to show elsewhere, in the development of the child's communication pattern the relation between emotion and expression of emotion is learnt before vocabulary and grammar; emotions, in English, are in the I.S. factors of language, so one would expect them to stay constant throughout utterances of a particular kind. Those under discussion being questions, then all questions should have these patterns.

THE SAME DISCUSSION WITH THREE WEST AFRICAN LANGUAGES

The three languages are Yoruba, Nupe and Ibo. The same procedure was carried out on all three occasions. First there was a thorough discussion of the situation in English with a group of the native-language speakers. They then produced an initial draft of the process in their mother tongue; this was discussed in a group. Then their findings were tested against a further group of native-language speakers for accuracy. I have taught in a school which was in a ratio of 3:1 Yoruba to Nupe. I am acquainted with the Ibo language through work and worship in Nigeria, and I have frequent contact with teachers from all three language groups who are on courses in the United Kingdom.

The function of I.S. is quite different in tonal languages (Pike 1946) where intonation across a *word* changes the meaning rather than intonation change across the *sentence*. However another function of I.S., more particularly the tone element, has quite a different function to English; this has been noted in the African languages where Nida (1957, p. 128) points out that with the Mongbandi of the northern part of the Congo (presumably the old name of the area as the evidence was published in 1950) the time of the action is indicated by the tone of the pronouns:

> *mbi* – I or *'e* – we

spoken with a low tone shows the past, spoken with a middle tone shows the present and spoken with a high tone shows the future. He also points out that in the two-register systems of many Bantu languages, the contrast in tone is required to differentiate the second person singular from the third person singular (Nida 1957, p. 113).

But I have not found any development of this promising start.

1. Yoruba

When we turn to Yoruba we find a very different state of affairs. Yoruba is spoken in the South West State of Nigeria, Kwara State and in adjoining Francophone territories. These people have a long, well-documented history, and there have been a number of studies about them. The language in particular is introduced in Ward (1952), Carnochan (1964, pp. 397–406) and in the publications of the Ministry of Education of the South West State, Nigeria.

As I have pointed out, in Yoruba intonation change across a *word* changes meaning, as opposed to English where intonation across the sentence changes meaning. This is most easily seen with an example:

owó	–	hand	high on last syllable
owò	–	reputable	low on last syllable
ówò	–	broom	rise on first, low on last

(I use the older orthography, the one I am most familiar with. The Government of the South West State have standardized a new and more accurate orthography.)

It is possible to make up sentences of apparently similar sounding words where the only change is the stress on the words, not an easy task for the English speaker, e.g.,

> *Òpòlópó òpòló ni kò ni opolo lori lópòlópò*
> Many frogs are devoid of reasoning.

Igba enia fi igbá ru ìgba
Two hundred people carried garden eggs in calabashes.

Because of this it is not always possible to inflect a sentence to show a change of meaning. If there is the rising sound on the last syllable of a word which is also the last syllable of a sentence, then the turning of a statement into a question is not usually possible. Taking the question 'Is Margaret going to wear that hat' which I used in my analysis of English, I then asked my Yoruba consultants how they would translate this into Yoruba to express anger, then impatience and finally incredulity or surprise. My first group included people from Ogbomoso who were generally deferred to as speaking the purest Yoruba. The work was then tested against a second group who included people from Lagos, Akure, Ijebu; they agreed with the first group. But as readers familiar with Yoruba will realize, there are local variants, as Yoruba still has many recognized dialects in stronger and weaker forms. All my correspondents agree that the outlines below are acceptable as – if I may use the phrase – 'standard received Yoruba'. As in the orthography of many African languages, the written form is far nearer the phonetic written form than in English. In the sentence, 'Margaret' becomes *'Magireti'* and 'hat' is translated *'gèlè'*. The vowels used should be given their Yoruba value, not the English.

(a)   When we come to the discussion of this sentence, showing anger directed at Margaret:

'Is MARGARET going to wear that hat?'

becomes   *Sé gèlè na ni Magireti nwe beyen*

1   2   3 4   5   6   7

1 'is', has a high pitch on the first word, the sort of pitch which is the result of physiological stress closing the throat and raising the voice.
2 'headtie'.
6 is the continuous form of the verb 'to wear'.
7 translates as 'in that way'. Thus the predicate of the sentence takes the stress.
The comparison with the English sentence is obvious.

(b)   When we come to surprise, incredulity:

'Is Margaret going to wear THAT hat?'
or, in a stronger form
'Is Margaret going to wear THAT HAT?'

We find in Yoruba

> *Sé bi Magireti na ti we gèlè yen niyen*
>
>   1 2   3   4 5 6 7 8 9

1 (*se*) – 'is' still starts the question.

3 (*Magireti*) – has moved to a position immediately behind the 'is'.

6 (*we*) – indicates a tense change; we now have the present infinitive of the verb 'to wear'.

7 (*gèlè*) – the word 'headtie' moves from behind the auxiliary verb to after the main verb.

8 and 9 (*yen niyen*) – substitutes for *beyen* to give much more emphasis; it has the literal translation of 'that, that condition' or 'that, that way', where the doubling of the word gives emphasis (as in making comparatives).

(c) For impatience

> 'IS Margaret going to wear that hat?'

we have the Yoruba form

> *Sé Magireti koi we gèlè na tan ni*
>
>   1   2   3 4 5 6 7 8

2 (*Magireti*) is still just after the auxiliary verb.

4 (*we*) – we still have the present infinitive of the verb 'to wear'.

5 and 6 give emphasis and also the idea that if something doesn't happen very soon the speaker will leave.

Intensity of emotion is related to loudness and to increased stress. But also, more in Yoruba than in English, by means of head movements, eye movements. At this stage of analysis, this is a complication that cannot be entered into.

Now I have shown that in English with questions of this kind emotions are identified by definable I.S. patterns associated with certain specific grammatical features:

1. anger is associated with the nominal component;
2. impatience is associated with the verbal component;
3. surprise is associated with the pronominal, where the surprise is caused by pronominal.

Contrasting this with Yoruba, we see that information carried by paralinguistic features in English have now moved up into tense change and word order. This pattern, as one would expect, follows a definite order:

Emotion	English	Yoruba
Anger	I.S. pattern on nominal	Continuous form of main verb. The pronominal equivalent of the English is next to the auxiliary verb. Stress on auxiliary verb.
Incredulity	I.S. pattern on pronominal	We have the present infinitive form of the main verb. The pronominal equivalent has been replaced by the nominal. Emphasis is strengthened by vocabulary change.
Impatience	I.S. pattern on the verbal component	of the nominal and pronominal. There are vocabulary changes.

The most important matter that comes out of this brief study is the principle that paralinguistic changes in English require vocabulary and grammatical changes in Yoruba. This is to be expected as the two languages utilize the I.S. structure in quite different ways.

At this stage in the research this can only be a crude analysis, and, as further work is done, these initial precepts may have to be modified. However, it emphasizes the need for further development of a grammar related to social intention which allows discoveries of this kind to be developed.

Status and solidarity. This exercise so far has only been conducted utilizing one of the three universals – emotion. What of status and solidarity? We have to start asking ourselves questions such as 'when can this be said', 'to whom' and 'in what circumstances'.

If we look at status we see that this sort of question is possible to a superior. It is, as it were, an attack; whether the speaker is being impatient, angry or incredulous he is commenting adversely on Margaret – she may well feel attacked, done down, criticized. This attack is possible when the speaker is in a superior position because only superiors can make overt attacks. The inferior might say this behind Margaret's back, in a situation where he knows that Margaret will not learn about it.

The other possible situation is when Margaret and the speaker are in a solidarity situation, i.e., are friends, or in a family situation. Being in a family does not preclude status nor does it automatically imply friendship; the term 'family' in the context of social grammar is almost meaningless as it gives so little information. For example, when I was asking my Yoruba correspondents about this question, without exception they thought in 'family' terms. They explored, albeit briefly, the womenfolk in the family to and about whom it could be said. This is one of the areas that needs investigating further because the Yoruba extended family is not only very different from the nuclear English family in size but also in orientation.

2. *Nupe*

The Nupe are a people astride the Niger River to the West before its junction with the Benue. They are politically divided between those who look to the Emir at Bida, north of the Niger, which was strongly influenced by the Fulani conquest of the North of Nigeria, and those who look to the Etsu Pategi the Ruler of Pategi, south of the Niger River. He claims to be the original Etsu Pategi and considers the Emir of Bida not to be of pure Nupe descent. The informants I used were from the Bida Emirate, and dialectical differences such as can be found at Agaie, Lafia, Lafiagi, etc., have been ignored.

The language is similar to Yoruba in that it has the three tones – high, medium and low – and also uses the same accents to indicate the low and the high tone:

    ebà   –   place,
    ebá   –   husband,
    èbà   –   fever.

(As it occurs in the text I also need to mention the nasalized vowel which occurs in both Yoruba and Nupe. For example, 'wucî' is pronounced with the 'u' nasalized and is sometimes written 'wuncin'. My informants preferred this latter orthography, and I have retained it.)

Again, like Yoruba, words of similar phonetic make-up can be used to create sentences, utilizing the tonal difference.

The English sentence –

'Is Margaret going to wear that hat?'

becomes:

    'Fùla wùncin ga Maggi à pe o?'
      1   2   3   4   5 6 7

1 'hat'.
2 'that'.
3 'going to'.
4 'Margaret'.
5 continuous form of 'to put on'.
6 'put on'.
7 a phatic utterance, which with 'a' tends to end all sentences.

This sentence can be either a statement or a question. The difference is the intonation of the last two syllables. In a statement *'pe o'* is made on a level medium note. In the question form there is a slur medium-high-medium over these two words.

Anger in Nupe is shown by increasing the speed of the utterance with an emphasis on 1 – *'fula'* meaning hat.

To express surprise, we get

  Nhun fùla wùncin ga Maggi à pe o

  1   2   3 4   5 6 7

1 *'nhun'* is a phatic utterance used to express surprise. The rest of the sentence stays the same as far as order is concerned, but we need emphasis on both *'nhun'* and *'fula'*.

  To express impatience we have the form
  Maggi la pe fula wùncin zo a
  1   2 3 4   5   6 7

This is a different word order and is a far stronger question than the previous ones:

  2 *'la'* is substituted for *'ga'* and shows that the speaker expected the completion of the action; 'has not' rather than 'going to'.
  6 *'zo'* is for emphasis and to show that the speaker will leave Margaret behind if she does not finish her actions immediately. One would expect Margaret to come out with the action completed or in the process of finishing.
  7 *'a'* replaces the *'o'* of the previous sentences.

The whole sense of this sentence has now changed and could well be given in English by:

  'Hasn't Margaret finished putting on that hat yet?'.

Once again the whole process is different from English, particularly in the use of phatic utterances:

Emotion	English	Nupe
Statement	Change of word order	Normal pattern
Question	I.S. pattern normal for question.	Medium-high-medium glide over verb infinitive and phatic utterance.
Anger	I.S. pattern on nominal.	Increasing speed, emphasis on the object of the sentence.

Emotion	English	Nupe
Incredulity	I.S. pattern on pronominal. Stronger emotion is given by strengthening I.S. features.	Introduction of phatic utterance in the initial position, plus emphasis on the utterance and object of question.
Impatience	I.S. pattern on verbal component.	Vocabulary changes with a change of meaning compared with English.

Once again we see that paralinguistic changes in English are not complemented by similar changes in Nupe. Once again it is obvious that the analysis is necessarily crude, but the point is made.

The last form of the Nupe is restricted to a high status speaker, whereas the others can be used in a greater range of social relationships.

3. Ibo

This is the language of the East Central State of Nigeria. The orthography is under review at this time, and I shall use that provided by my informants, that of Union Ibo. As usual with these languages we have the familiar feature of tone change over the meanings of words:

akwá	–	cloth	*ákwa*	–	egg
akwa	–	cry	*akwà*	–	bed

Moving to our familiar sentence 'Is Margaret going to wear that hat' we find the following patterns. For anger we have:

Amaghim Ka Margaret g'esi kpue okpu ahu

    1   2   3   4   5   6   7

1 'unconceivable', shows surprise as well as anger; the emphasis on *'ama...'* rather than upon *'ghim'* which defines the concern expressed by the first pronoun I rather idiomatically implied.
2 'how' shows the right of Margaret to wear that hat.
4 'would' is a short form of *'ga-esi'* and is usually so shortened to stress and to qualify the objective noun.
5 'wear' strictly used to show something worn on the head only.
6 'hat'.
7 'that' in the nominative.

We come to surprise and have the form:

Obú Margaret ga ekpu okpu ahu?
  1   2   3   4   5   6

1 'is' the question form, introducing a subject. The stress and high
  tone on the second syllable.
3 'to' or 'going' with emphasis on *'ga'*, expressing inquisitiveness.
4 'wear', the present infinitive.

Finally impatience:

Ojurum-anya na Margaret ga ekpu okpu ahu
    1   2 3   4   5   6   7   8

1 and 2 'I am surprised' with the meaning of disappointment.
3 'that' or 'and' but used here as a link between the relative pronoun
  conjugated in *'ojurum anya'*, and the subject Margaret.
5 'would' or 'is going to' used as an adverb.
6 'to wear'.

Once again we have a very different pattern to the English utterance.
Because of the different usage of I.S. patterns the information in the
paralinguistic features has moved into lexis and grammar.

Emotion	English	Ibo (Igbo)
Anger	I.S. pattern on the nominal.	Emphasis on adverb of manner indicates anger.
Incredulity	I.S. pattern on pronominal. Stronger emotion given by strengthening I.S. features.	New lexical features and tense change to present from conditional.
Impatience	I.S. pattern on the verbal component.	Further lexical changes. Tense still in the present.

At this moment in time I am quite frustrated by the minimal information in the column under the heading *Ibo*. There must be a pattern to
these changes, but I no longer have access to Ibo speakers who are
sufficiently experienced in language study to analyze their own utterances.

DISCUSSION

If we draw up a table as in Figure 2 and compare it with descriptions of
sound patterns in tonal languages such as chosen in Dunstan (1969) the

Figure 2.

Emotion	English	Yoruba	Nupe	Ibo/Igbo
Anger	I.S. Pattern on the nominal	Continuous form of the main verb. The pronominal equivalent of .the English is next to the auxiliary verb. Stress on auxiliary verb.	Increasing speed, emphasis on the object of the sentence.	Emphasis on adverb of manner indicates anger.
Incredulity Surprise	I.S. pattern on pronominal. Stronger emotion is given by strengthening I.S. features.	We have the present infinitive form of the main verb. The pronominal equivalent has been replaced by the nominal. Emphasis is strengthened by vocabulary change.	Introduction of phatic utterance in the initial position, plus emphasis on the utterance and object of question.	New lexical features and tense change to present from conditional.
Impatience	I.S. pattern on the verbal component.	The verb is the same as are the positions of the nominal and pronominal. There are vocabulary changes.	Vocabulary changes with a change of meaning compared with English.	Further lexical changes; tense still in the present.

differences in approach are very obvious. I am dealing with social-functional relationships as opposed to internal relationships. The implications of this I discuss in the next chapter.

The type of description which I am attempting is required to provide the basis for the other part of social grammar – 'who is permitted to say these things and in what circumstances?' Obviously I have only just started to outline ground rules. For example, in the Nupe situation there is an extreme of impatience that is not strictly equivalent to the whole range of I.S. intensity of the English utterance. I can be impatient with Margaret by saying:

'Is Margaret going to wear that hat?'

without having any effect on Margaret; she does not bother to hurry. But I can also say it with the same word order and more emphasis (sic), which will make her take action. Now what is the difference between these two utterances? Where does Margaret glean the information that allows her to have a choice of two actions? How does she know that in case one she has time to dawdle some more, whereas in the second case she has to come out at once? Is there something subtle in the I.S. or does it lie in the social context? Is an observer aware of this difference of choice? Or might it not be most likely that we have a series based on my basic analysis:
1. that there is an I.S. pattern which in a given status situation allows us to discriminate between a request, an order and absolute imperative;
2. that the order, and imperative are modified by the personal relationship.

My ubiquitous observer will go through a two-stage process: in the first stage he listens to the utterance and makes the decision that this normally expresses an order, a request, etc.; the second stage takes in the social context and says that now the request becomes an order or vice-versa.

When we move over to Nupe we have first to decide if there is the subtlety of expression in Nupe. Just how complex is the range that can be expressed in Nupe and to what social categories can they be attached?

When we look at these broad categories of status, solidarity and emotion we can, as the second stage of analysis, take both sociological and anthropological descriptions as subclasses, e.g., social class or kinship terms. We can go on to analyze how far solidarity is possible and how far it affects language. I think that we must always be aware of the third party in this activity – the other members of the society under discussion who make their own value judgments about the behaviour of the people they are listening to and watching. Then, outside that, as it were, is the dispassionate uninvolved observer who sees the anomalies of the judgments of the observers. The final stage is that of the sociologist or social anthropologist and the social grammarian who are theoretically completely outside the society.

For any social grammatical description to succeed it must work both ways; that is, it must be able to distinguish the language from the situation or the situation from the language. Given a language pattern we should be able to derive the social situations in which this utterance can be made; listening to the language patterns we should be able to distinguish the social situations in which they may be uttered.[28]

Finally, in this section all I have been able to do is to make out the outlines of the situation in the crudest way. Obviously each one of the languages dealt with needs its own complete analysis before any real comparison can be made. However I am confident that I have made the case for a radically different description of language and also that I have shown that intonation, stress, timbre, etc., are communication features capable of functional description which allows them to be codified and related to grammatical and lexical features in other languages.

We need a social grammar, and we need language descriptions which allow us to describe language as a social and personal function. I do wish to emphasize the importance of the individual in the language process. Social categories may lay down the basic prescriptions but as the individual changes society and is changed by society, so language can be changed by the individual as can the language usage. With Lapiere I am more inclined to the idea of the individual effects on change rather than on evolutionary, utopian pressures lying in economic or scientific immutable forces:

> ... social change is worked by the efforts of individuals – functioning in various capacities as innovators, advocates or adopters – who have in some specific respect been freed from the conventionalizing effects of social ideology and of organizational membership (Lapiere 1965).

---

28. There is a descriptive difficulty here. We have to distinguish between what is socially permitted and what a person is driven to saying in extremes of emotion or stress.

CHAPTER IV

Summary: Answers and Implications

I postulate the need for a social grammar which will enable us to classify language in such a way that we can provide a description of language which allows us to describe just what can be said, by which person, in which situation and to which other person in any particular society; a social grammar which allows us to make value judgments of the variety:

'Isn't he angry'
'She's rude'
'They're happy'
'He's asking for trouble'.

To do this I suggest that we have to describe language as it functions within society. I take three relationships from society and individuals in society – those of status, solidarity and emotion – and show how language is initially determined by the social superior who has power of one kind or other and then show that this determining power is modified by first solidarity and finally by emotion. I point out that in this line of approach language needs a functional description which I show as differing from grammatical description and is dependent upon functions in society. The initial analysis covers questions, commands, negatives, abuse, comments and responses. At this stage only the first four can be defined with any clarity. This analysis is set in, rather than derived from, the view of knowledge being socially based. Reification, whilst almost inevitable, eventually ossifies any study, and this has occurred in linguistic schools. Lack of grammatical fit, for example, is suggested to be a function of reification rather than a reflection of any language reality.

As a further contribution to the forging of tools for social grammatical analysis and description I show that the function of that group of paralinguistic features subsumed under the symbol of I.S. is assumed to be paralinguistic in English but that this function moves to lexis and grammar in some tonal languages from West Africa. At this point in time there is available only the crudest evidence; there lie ahead years of research.

In the many years I have been concerned with developing and formulating the concept of a social grammar I have found no one with similar ideas (apart from Burling's (1970) book *Man's Many Voices*). However, as I read the work of sociolinguists I found myself in a somewhat dream-like situation. One read the works and happily one was travelling a familiar road and saying 'Yes, yes, this is what I think; yes I am with this'. Then suddenly one has left the familiar road and is travelling in a strange country with all the familiar landmarks gone. This disorientation was disturbing because, like any academic worker. I wanted a 'home', the place where I could obtain a degree of academic respectability. Whilst I quickly realized that I was working on a new frontier, nevertheless it was some time before I realized the essential difference between my work and that of sociolinguists.

We are both concerned with language as a social activity, but the sociolinguist thinks of himself as a sociologist and whilst exploring social relationships and language he relies on current linguistic descriptions. I am saying 'Yes, that must be done, but also we must develop new descriptions of language and show up new relationships between language and society'. I repeat a part of the quotation from Burling from my introduction:

... I am not primarily concerned with the internal structure of language, but only with the way that structure is affected by and dependent upon things other than language (Burling 1970).

If a social grammar can be developed then it ought to serve as a tool for sociolinguists. Indeed it is necessary for the study of society, the individual and language that fixed bounds be *not* fixed; that whilst there is a centre of interest there are no boundaries; that *fields* of knowledge do not imply hedges and walls.

One of the most interesting workers in the field of sociolinguistics is J.J. Gumperz. He started as a science graduate, obtained a Ph.D. in linguistics and through his work as an anthropologist has become a major figure in the field of sociolinguistics. A brief look at his book *Language in Social Groups* (1971) will underline the difference of approach. He discusses social interaction and suggests that social relationships refer to regular patterns of interaction. He lists some of these as father-son, salesman-customer, husband-wife, etc. But these are not concrete in themselves; they vary from culture to culture and even from subculture to subculture, e.g., the husband-wife relationship does not always imply that the husband is always superior. I am arguing that there is a fundamental relationship of status with inferior and superior and that the dominant figure – the one with the high status – has power over the other and that it will be shown in language. If we know the status initiation and response patterns in any language then we can determine the status relationship between two speakers. It might be that normally the husband has dominance according to the local subculture pattern, but in listening we hear that the woman is using the dominant patterns, and we draw social conclusions and express them in language:

'That poor fellow is hen-pecked'.

But of course the observer may not be the involvement-free anthropologist, but a member of the society who makes the value judgment:

'That man is being put in his proper position; his wife is maintaining woman's rights'.

In the same section Gumperz discusses certain binary semantic choices – 'dine-eat', 'talk-lecture' and points out that whilst they share some features they differ in some specific features. He says:

Alternation of this type may thus be viewed from two perspectives. In the realm of semantics it selects among sub-classes of referents. In the sphere of social interaction it reflects the position actors wish to assume relative to each other, i.e., the quality of their relationships. Whenever a set of linguistic forms is interchangeable within the same frame without significant change in meaning, it is the second aspect which becomes most important. In the course of any one encounter mutual relationships are constantly defined and redefined in accordance with the speaker's ultimate aim. But each encounter sets bounds to this type of variation. Social restraints on language choice express the norms of defining such bounds. If he violates these, the actor risks misunderstanding (Gumperz 1971, p. 155).

Social grammar is concerned with the bounds and the classifying of the social restraints of language and the relations between these and the forms of communication and as such seeks for universals that will allow for change in society and comparison between societies. Status is one such broad classification, as is emotion.

Further on in the same chapter the discussion continues about the variety of styles. My analysis of this situation would suggest that these styles are capable of being plotted on a continuum of status at various points:

1. gross society   3. village society
2. regional society   4. family society.

Social grammar would define those elements in utterances which would allow the observer to define the different statuses claimed by the different actors and to make evaluations about the acceptability of their own perceived role and that of the other participants.

In Chapter 16 (p. 274), Gumperz uses traditional linguistic forms to analyze the differences between two groups in Norway. In social grammar one would ask a further series of questions. Do the two groups show emotions in different ways? How do they modify status by solidarity? What emotions are permitted in what social situations? If there are different answers for the two groups then the analysis would go on to find out where in the communication process the difference lies.

Finally, to show the difference I take a quotation from the conclusion of this chapter:

> In interactional sociolinguistics, therefore, we can no longer base our analyses on the assumption that language and society constitute different kinds of reality, subject to correlational studies. Social and linguistic information is comparable only when studied within the same general analytical frame work. Moving from statements of social constraints to grammatical rules this represents a transformation from one level of abstraction to another within a single communicative system (Gumperz 1971, p. 305).

The first point is of course that 'linguistic' needs a much wider meaning; the so-called paralinguistic features are part of the descriptive apparatus of a social grammar. However, more importantly, at this stage in my thought I would suggest that in social grammar we are not effecting a transformation from one level to another but that we are developing a single description of a communicative system. Gumperz goes on to say that the paper he has presented

> ... demonstrates the importance of social or non-referential meaning for the study of language in society. Mere naturalistic observation of speech behaviour is not enough. In order to interpret what he hears the investigator must have some background knowledge of the local culture, of the processes which generate social meaning (1971, p. 305).

And I would add: Yes, and he mus be able to classify this local knowledge against universals which are to be found in the fundamental nature of society and of man himself.

ANSWERS

In the introduction I suggested two questions that provoked this study. At last I suggest answers. Why couldn't I know if people were angry or not? Because the carriers of this information are not the same as in English. In English we use I.S. factors; the Yoruba require lexical and grammatical changes. Why do Yoruba students find it more difficult to learn English than do Hausa students? Because, though Hausa does have words that change meaning with the tone level, nevertheless Hausa inflects over the sentence and can change meaning using I.S. systems. So basically Hausa students have less work to do and also do not have to learn a brand new set of concepts.

IMPLICATIONS

1. Social grammar

One of the criteria for evaluating a new theory is to see if it generates information for further study and whether it feeds into other areas of knowledge. Under the first head there is a mass of work to do. In English there is a need to follow through the implications of the relationship of I.S. patterns to grammatical features. Is the emotion of anger associated with the nominal in *all* questions (as opposed to certain questions)? There obviously must be consistency, but how complex is the consistency? Will the analysis of the question series produce a simple pattern or a series of complex patterns? Are these patterns related to any of the social determinants? When we come to the other categories how far can we rely on our analysis of questions? Where, if at all, is there a borderline between impatience and anger? Because in real life impatience and anger can be closely related and merge into one another, will there be 'grey' areas where there will be alternate classifications according to the observer's own social position?

There remains all the work to do with the classification of emotions – which show in speech and how are they shown? I have mentioned already the list of adverbs of manners and emotions which have been derived from behaviour. Just what, in utterances, allow us to make these judgments?

Emotion leads us back to solidarity and status. Here we have decisions about subdivisions and the possibility of different ways of looking at social stratification and also the approach from different disciplines. If we consider English society from a class division, how do we include kinship relationships? How does language reveal not only social class but regional or job differences?

Returning to the language classifications: there are the areas already introduced – negatives (refusals), commands, abuse, etc. As we classify by social intention we have the whole nomenclature problem. Do we persist with old grammatical terms differentiated by typographical distinctions or should new terms be invented? If we take traditional grammar as anatomy and social grammar as physiology, then we have to build up descriptions concerned not only with traditional grammar as a discrete discipline, and social grammar as a discrete discipline, but terms which allow us to discuss the interdependence of the two.

With regard to negatives: is it just a power situation which determines refusal or are there different refusal patterns for different social sub-groups? The boundary line between order and request is another 'grey' area. Many social misjudgments are made and apologies demanded because a request has been interpreted as an order. It may well be that the examination of this in terms of social grammar might reveal more about the individual social perceptions than about language itself. This brings forward whether we can have a single social grammar for English; might there not be a whole range of social grammars dealing with different subgroups but which, if presented as a whole series of Venn diagrams, might have areas of overlap?

Abuse is an intriguing area. To abuse someone you must utilize material that is significant to a particular social group. The words 'you fool' can be said in English in a number of different ways to provoke reactions from laughter through to attempts at physical violence. Just which I.S. factors are associated with what social conditions to allow of this variety of reactions? Why is it vulgar but 'normal' to say:

'Oh, fuck off you fucking bastard'

but a little amusing to say:

'Oh, sexually intercourse off, you sexually intercoursing illegitimate'.

But also how can I, as in individual, know how to use the latter phrase as verbal weapon to put down someone, using the laughter and the moment of incomprehension whilst the phrase was worked out to leave the room in a dominant position?[29] The whole basis of abuse words

---

29. The use of this word 'fuck' is worthy of a small paper. For example, the sentence 'Some fucking fucker's fucked the fucking fucker up' (even written down without I.S. patterns being indicated) carries a great deal of meaning. Why? Where are the information carriers? How do you analyse this in transformational terms – what are the deep and surface structures? How is it that people who have never heard the sentence, far less used it, immediately grasp its meaning? We have 'break up' meaning to destroy and break into pieces; but 'fuck up' and 'cock up' meaning to break down in the sense of being unserviceable – why?

seems to be social – but abuse is carried in the I.S. pattern in English, as well.

'Go away' he said insultingly;
'This is a sort of coffee' he said insultingly.

Where, in other languages, does this insult occur? Just how did a particular I.S. pattern become insulting? Because an inferior is using a superior's phrase to a superior? Is it socially possible for an inferior to develop abuse and be insulting? Was the definition of an insult originally in the eye, or ear, of the superior?

The questions seem endless. At this stage I suggest they are right and proper and are an indication of a fruitful theory.

2. Sociolinguistics

I have already suggested that social grammar will add a new dimension to the study of language in society. It does this in two ways. First socially speaking it gives some universals which will allow a preliminary analysis of the social situation which affects any particular group in relation to another group. Secondly, it gives another type of linguistic description to the sociolinguistic tool-box. For example, Bernstein in his works (1960a, 1960b, 1962a, 1962b, 1967, 1972) together with those who have developed his ideas (Lawton 1968, Robinson 1965a, 1965b, 1972; but see Williams 1970) have suggested that the social structure creates a code, and the code affects the way in which a person perceives the world, forms concepts about it and expresses his perceptions and concepts. Accepting the criticism that these show different groups rather than that one group is necessarily deprived in the sense of lacking what the other group has, this analysis makes sense. However the original work suggested that the choices people made lay in four areas:

(a) lexical differences
(b) grammatical structure differences
(c) lower information content and higher predictability in the restricted code
(d) the use of more introductory and final phrases in the restricted code.

The choice one had was, in the original statement of the theory, limited for those with a working class background, and therefore one had a restricted code. Contrariwise, the middleclass speaker had an elaborated code. I do not propose to discuss the various criticisms and developments but purely to show first that this choice may be because the social situation limits the possibility of utterance – the restricted code user is restricted, not so much because of his own limitations but because, being different and in some sense status inferior, he just doesn't use the elaborated code. Thus alternance is not only a property of an utterance, but it may be a function of the speaker. A speaker's alternance is determined not only by what choice he knows but what choices the situation allows him to use. My contribution is to draw attention to the function of paralinguistic features particularly when they are classified in relation to society, and at least add another dimension for analysis. It seems also that not enough distinction is made between social failure in language and systematic failure in language (see Williams 1970). There needs to be more careful investigation so that we can distinguish between what is lack of language, i.e., being below a standard through lack of grammar and lexis, and the time where an appropriate utterance has not been used due to social position, perhaps lack of social grammar awareness or where 'appropriate' is defined solely by the usage of a dominant group which in the past has denied particular language patterns to an inferior status group (cf. language expectations of the Southern-state white man with regard to Negroes). A social grammarian would analyze language in relation to status, solidarity, etc., and thus create the conditions for a more accurate and subtle discussion of the function of class in the language situation. This would, I suggest, lead us away from discussion in purely social-class terms and toward more awareness of other status situations which affect language choice.

3. Language development

I have to some degree discussed this (page 53 ff.). We realize now that a child is learning language patterns related to a whole variety of social and individual relationships and that these lie not only in vocabulary and word order but in the so-called paralinguistic features. So, for the proper understanding of the child's development, we must have a categorizing of language as social function – and this is what social grammar sets out to do. With a reasonable grammar we would be able to derive information about the child's early language experience by examining the social relationships of language revealed in his utterance. And of course the reverse of this – we should be able to build up areas of expertise and lack of expertise when we have a proper analysis of status, etc., in a variety of roles, and not just that of social class. Further, we should be able to do this across cultures and subcultures.

One of the research areas in the growth of language in the young child is that of the internalization of reality in the development of language. I have at least shown that this is more than a matter of vocabulary and grammar; it is also an internalizing of social relationships as they are expressed in utterances. The child learns all the information-carrying patterns of I.S. and their usage and their references to himself (and between himself and significant others!) All this is taken in and related not only in agreement with grammatical and lexical items but also with the contradictions between the I.S. pattern and the grammatical and lexical patterns *and* those set in status, solidarity and emotional situations.

This naturally leads on to suggest new ideas about that omnibus but diffuse label 'deprivation'. A child who observes and experiences only a limited area of social relationships will only have a language pattern reflecting these limited areas. For example, if we have a child brought up in a fatherless home whose mother only has female friends, and then this child goes to an infant school with only female teachers, he may reach the age of nearly eight before he has anything but the most limited experience of child/man, woman/man, man/man relationships. From a social grammar point of view we can see that he might have no idea how to express the variety of emotions in the status/solidarity situations other than woman/child, woman/woman, thus being deprived of a large area of language experience. Yet he might well perform as well as a middleclass child, and his deprivation be quite hidden. As a working class child he might also have a double loss measured against the double standard of sexually mixed society and 'middle-class' standards. A similar child brought up in an extended family would have a different and fuller appreciation of the relationships of language and society. By insisting on the term 'status' we also can move away from the preoccupation with the class system in English and be aware of other superior/inferior situations.

By insisting upon an analysis of language as individual and social behaviour we can see more accurately the function of language in children's social and intellectual development as well as language development. By looking at the status structures in subcultures in England and their expression in language we can develop perhaps a variety of language programmes in order that a subgroup can more clearly understand another group.

At the moment I can do no more than suggest possibilities, and one I would suggest is that the whole of classroom language would benefit from a social-grammar approach. This was hinted at in my discussion of grammatical fit, and I have had no opportunity of studying in this area. But the reality of human relationships as opposed to the appearance is often revealed in language. I have mentioned two cases in my own experience where a knowledge of social language patterns had to be discovered before any solution could be attempted. In the case of the junior school boy who required a slap to cue him to action on adult orders, it was the appreciation of horizontal and vertical language that suggested a solution.

It is regrettable that these points sound so repetitious, but the contribution of social grammar is similar in all the parts of this section – that of a radically different view of language extending our horizon and suggesting new relationships and classifications.

4. Language teaching

A. *Mother-tongue learning.* I suggest that the main importance is, in the first instance, in mother-tongue learning awareness on the part of teachers. Since my first tentative formulations I have developed my ideas with, and on, practising teachers who have gone to their classrooms and found them fruitful. The biggest conceptual breakthrough comes when the teacher grasps that language is a behaviour pattern that is closely related to social behaviour. My analysis of status, solidarity and emotion have been used by teachers to sort out all sorts of relationships, particularly in mixed communities with a mobile population. Take an extreme example: suppose you have children from a tight coal mining community who find themselves in school with children from a Liverpool dockside background (in a new town, for example). On the one hand we have girls who come from a matrilinear society and on the other those who come from a patrilinear family. The dock children are used to the dominance of the woman – the idea that the man takes the wage packet home and receives pocket money and that the wife's mum is round the corner with Aunty Beth, etc., near at hand. The children learn a very definite pattern of behaviour which will show itself in language – ideas of politeness, what are feasible utterances in defined situations, what is due in the various male/female roles. The miner's children come from a society where Dad is far more authoritative, where he decides what is the right amount of housekeeping, where social life is governed by Dad's desires and those of his few mates from the coalface gang. Here we have a very different expression of language for the social roles. Not only the children but the teacher will listen to utterances and make value judgments of politeness and rudeness, etc., where the children are intending something quite different. A proper social grammar of the utterances of these two groups, even in a coarse form, might well help social understanding in the classroom.

As a last brief comment: we have had in English a mode of language for an adult/child which is basically an almost institutionalized form of language. The child is in an inferior situation, indeed in a powerless situation, and we as adults behave as high-status operators – politeness, etc., are at our discretion. Eventually our children grow up and have to take up a whole variety of roles in the status continuum; a well-thought-out social grammar might well help us to understand the changes involved in utterances and make us more aware of when childhood ends and adulthood begins. It may well allow us to devise ways of reducing our intergeneration tensions.

B. *Second-language and foreign-language teaching.* The difference between these two I see is that in the former the child has to learn a new language in order to succeed in education and society. With the latter he is learning a new language for social convenience or because the education authorities decree it. The difference between the two is in degree rather than method. The second language situation is more intense, with more highly motivated teachers and learners, for example.

Of course the whole of this study grew out of my need as a teacher of English as a second language in Nigeria. It is the first attempt to forge a tool to examine the differences between English and tonal languages in a way that is more meaningful to teacher and students. I am sure that I have started on the road to success. It is more meaningful to show that a certain I.S. pattern in English is related to the expression of anger and that this is or is not permissible – in particular status, solidarity situations – than to ask students to remember the pages of rules derived from patterns of weak and strong stresses working from the beginning or the end of the sentence. If you are using language as a social function, a description of it as a social function is more directly relevant than a description of it as reified form.

The comments in section A above are equally relevant here. Properly developed, a social grammar can do nothing but good in the field of language teaching whether mother-tongue, second or foreign.

C. *The study of the nature of society.* It is with diffidence that I discuss .this area of study subsuming as it does sociology, social anthropology and ethnoscience amongst others. Social grammar dealing as it does with matters such as status, solidarity and friendship, and the interpretation of these in value judgments such as politeness, authority, rudeness, lese-majesty, insolence, deference, can but help our descriptions of society. Important items such as kinship terms may well be recategorized in terms of status, etc., and the language patterns derived, and these patterns related in turn to other status conditions.

For example, in Yoruba the word *baba* is used as title for all the maternal male relationships of the mother's generation and preceding. It is also extended to cover males in authority in other areas. Are there subtleties of use by combining it with special grammatical features or I.S. features which would allow a more discriminate usage? Is there a gradation of respect?

It is important to know in cross-cultural situations what can and cannot be said, in order to avoid offence. We are aware of broad language differences such as the full use of names in Russian which would at least be odd in English, the American habit of suggesting informality by the use of initials or forenames, the English custom of retaining the 'Mr.' or other titles. Yet there is rarely doubt that when the superior *allows* the use of a forename, thus actually abandoning his status situation, the observer is aware of it and acts accordingly in the language situation. However there are less well-defined differences. In English the close of a sentence is the plagual cadence or perfect cadence. When we want to assume an authoritative voice we change this pattern; even though we use a polite form of words, we finish on the mediant. In Ibo many sentences finish on the mediant, and it depends not upon the social intention but upon the meaning of the word. We then get a very subtle sort of mother-tongue interference. The listening Englishman hears an Ibo speaking English. Many, if not most, of his sentences finish not with the polite cadences but with the more common Ibo mediant; this is of course an authoritative voice in English. The Englishman makes a social judgment about the Ibo's relations with him. The judgment that the Ibo is being impolite is a false one. This occurred particularly in the days when the English and Ibo first came into general contact, for then the Ibo was in a status-inferior position and was using a form not permitted to an inferior. Generally by 1950 when I first went out to Nigeria the Ibo had the reputation of being cheeky and bumptious and of not knowing his place, and much of this judgment was based on social intercourse through language. However hard the Ibo tried to be polite he rarely succeeded! It is not the subject of this work to explore this field more here and now, but I believe I have done enough to show that social grammar has a tremendous contribution to this field of cross-cultural relationships.

As social grammar has to do with social relationships it should be a tool of use to sociologists; it should allow them to gain more accurate descriptions of social groups from an analysis of their language functioning. And it may help them to look at social change and not only social forms as at any one moment in time. A thorough analysis of grammatical fit will show not only the changes needed in language nomenclature but will shed some light on social change. We are aware of individual words moving up and down the social scale; we are far less aware of what changes in utterances are related to changes in social judgment as to what is, and is not, polite. An examination of armed forces language may well be revealing of the language possibilities of the times when armed forces society was institutionalized.

D. *Linguistic disciplines.* It is with even more diffidence that I approach this area of study. But it should be obvious that social grammar is related to other varieties of grammar and even that many grammatical terms have their origins in function rather than in form. However, I suggest that by showing that information carried in I.S. in English moves into grammar and lexis in other languages I have added another dimension to the direct study of language. Transformational grammarians will have to take into account the growth of awareness of social relationships having a language form and even more important, perhaps, the growth of emotional expression and its control in differing social situations.

Chapter 3 is the brief introduction to the comparison of English, Yoruba, Nupe and Ibo, and shows the contribution possible to comparative linguists. But I think there is also a tool to develop more information for comparative linguists who are interested in the development and movement of language. If we can classify the function not only of I.S. as a whole but of different sections of it, then we may well be able to draw up tables of those who use certain aspects for particular functions, and thus derive family trees. *A priori* it would be useful to assume that languages which use this or that part of an utterance to reveal a particular relationship may be related to other languages with a similar pattern. Given enough patterns we would reinforce or disagree with conclusions made by analysis of forms. By turning to anthropologists for additional evidence, and by making these language results available to anthropologists, we ought to shed light on the origins of language and movements of languages across countries and continents; and, to be not too speculative, we might come across information which would help in language change and development. I have hinted at this already when I discussed the origin and development of cow and beef from a common source. As social grammar relates language and society, changes in society will show as changes in language; as we have a history of social change we have a limited history of language change. I say limited for two reasons: (1) our history is written and the subtleties of the spoken word are lost;[30] (2) history has largely been written by the

30. If the full range of I.S. were capable of written expression, how limited would be the activity of directors and actors in the interpretation of Shakespeare!

status superior, so the status-inferior utterances may have had biased and very limited reporting. However all this will depend upon more work being done on the basic outline of a social grammar.

CONCLUSION

I envisage social grammar as being an additional tool for disciplines involving language. How this is done will depend upon the workers in the disciplines. The basic point to grasp is that here is *another* way of looking at and classifying languages which will add to our knowledge of language and communication and the societies in which language operates.

I have outlined the main approach and shown how it works in a coarse sort of way. There is a tremendous amount of work to be done in various fields in order to develop even a full outline of a social grammar of English. Very probably this will not be done except by the efforts of a partnership between different branches of linguistic study – phonologists, grammarians, historical linguistics, for example, with sociologists, anthropologists and teachers.

References

This bibliography contains references to two kinds of books – those which I have referred to in the text, and those which either have been fruitful in my thinking or which deal with theoretical postulates germane to my work. I have left out books which I have read but which are of little but marginal interest. There are very few periodicals referred to because, whilst articles give up-to-date information about work in a particular field, there is nothing to do with social grammar, and my research needed basic approaches rather than consideration of up-to-date workings of any particular field.

Abercrombie, D. (ed.) (1964), *In Honour of Daniel Jones.* Atlantic Highlands, N.J., Humanities Press.
– (1967), *Elements of General Phonetics.* University Press.
– (1968), 'Paralanguage', *British Journal of Disorders of Communication* 3(1).
Abravanel, Eugene (1962), 'A formal extension of the concept of role'. Master's thesis, Swarthmore.
Alatis, James (ed.) (1970), *Bilingualism and Language Contact: Anthropological, Linguistic, Psychological and Sociological Aspects.* Monograph Series on Languages and Linguistics, 23. Washington, D.C., Georgetown University Press.
Allen, J. P. B., and Van Buren, P. (1971), *Chomsky: Selected Readings.* Oxford, Oxford University Press.
Ardener, E. (ed.) (1971), *Social Anthropology and Language.* London, Tavistock Publications.
Argyle, M., and Lee, V. (eds.) (1972), *Social Relationships.* Open University.
Armstrong, L., and Ward, I.C. (1931), *Handbook of English Intonation.* 2nd ed. Cambridge, Heffer.
Austin, J.L. (1965), *How To Do Things with Words,* ed. by J. O. Urmson. New York, Oxford University Press.

Bach, Emmon (1964), *An Introduction to Transformational Grammar.* London, Holt, Rinehart & Winston.
Bach, E., and Harms, R. T. (1968), *Universals in Linguistic Theory.* London, Holt, Rinehart & Winston.
Barth, F. (1966), 'Models of social organizations'. Occasional Paper No. 33. London, Royal Anthropological Institute.

Beck, S. J. (1953), 'The science of personality: nomothetic or idiographic?', *The Psychological Review* 60.

Berger, P., and Luckman, T. (1966), *The Social Construction of Reality.* Garden City, N.Y., Doubleday.

Berger, P. L., and Berger, B. (1972), *Sociology: A Biographical Approach.* New York, Basic Books.

Berkowitz, L. (ed.) (1969), *Advances in Experimental Social Psychology.* New York, Academic Press Inc.

Bernstein, B. (1960a), 'Language and social class', *British Journal of Sociology,* Sept.

- (1960b), 'Social structure, language and learning', *Educational Research* 3(1):163–76.

- (1962a), 'Linguistic codes: hesitation phenomena and intelligence', *Language and Speech* 5, Jan.–March:31–45.

- (1962b), 'Social class, linguistic codes and grammatical elements', *Language and Speech* 5, Oct.–Dec.

- (1967), 'Elaborated and restricted codes: an outline', *International Journal of American Linguistics* 33(4), Part II.

- (1972), *Class, Code and Control.* London, Routledge & Kegan Paul.

Bertalanffy, Ludwig van (1968), *Psychology in the Modern World.*

Birdwhistell, Ray L. (1970), *Kinesics and Context.* Philadelphia, University of Pennsylvania Press.

Bogardus, E. S. (n.d.), 'Social distance and its origin', *Journal of Applied Sociology* 9:216-26.

Bonser, K. J. (1970), *The Drovers.* London, Macmillan.

Brandis, W., and Henderson, D. (1970), *Social Class, Language and Communication.* London, Routledge & Kegan Paul.

Bright, W. (1966), 'Sociolinguistics', *Proceedings of the U. C. L. A. Sociolinguistic Conference, 1964.* The Hague, Mouton.

Brower, R. A. (ed.) (1959), *On Translation.* Cambridge, Mass., Harvard University Press (New York, Oxford University Press, 1966).

Brown, Roger W. (1958), *Words and Things.* Glencoe, Ill., Free Press.

- (1965), *Social Psychology.* Glencoe, Ill., Free Press.

Brown, R., and Ford, M. (1961), 'Address in American English', *Journal of Abnormal and Social Psychology,* 62(2): 375-385.

Bryson, L., Finkelstein, L., Hoagland, H., and McIver, R. M. (eds.) (1955), *Symbols and Society.* New York, Harper.

Burling, Robbins (1970), *Man's Many Voices: Language in its Cultural Context.* New York, Holt, Rinehart & Winston.

Carmichael, L. (ed.) (1954), *Manual of Child Psychology.* New York, Wiley.

Carnochan, J. (1964), 'Pitch, tone and intonation in Yoruba', in: *In Honour of Daniel Jones,* ed. by L. D. Abercrombie. Atlantic Highlands, N.J., Humanities Press.

Carroll, J. B. (1964), *Language and Thought.* Englewood Cliffs, N.J., Prentice-Hall.

Cheek, Donald B. (1968), *Human Growth*. Philadelphia, Lea and Febiger.
Chomsky, N. (1965), *Aspects of the Theory of Syntax*. Cambridge, Mass., M.I.T. Press.
– (1968), *Language and Mind*. New York, Harcourt, Brace & World.
– (1972), *Problems of Knowledge and Freedom*. London, Barrie & Jenkins,
Chomsky, N. and Halle, N. (1968), *The Sound Pattern of English*. New York, Harper and Row.
Church, J. (1961), *Language and the Discovery of Reality*. New York, Random House.
Cicourel, Aaron Victor (1973), *Cognitive Sociology: Language and Meaning in Social Interaction*. Harmondsworth, Penguin.
Cole, L. R. (1967), 'Applied linguistics and the problem of meaning', *Audio-Visual Language Journal* 4(3).
Cooper, D. E. (1973), 'Grammar and the possession of concepts', *Proceedings of the Philosophy of Education Society of Great Britain* 7(2), July.
Crane, D. (1967), 'The gate-keepers of science. Some factors affecting the selection of articles for scientific journals', *American Sociologist* 4(2):195–201.
Crystal, D. (1969), *Prosodic Systems and Intonation in English*. Cambridge, Cambridge University Press.
Crystal, D., and Quirk, R. (1964), *Systems of Prosodic and Paralinguistic Features in English*. The Hague, Mouton.
Crystal, D., and Davy (1969), *Investigating English Style*. London, Longmans, Green & Co.

Darwin, C. (1965), *The Expression of the Emotions in Man and Animals*. London, Phoenix Books.
Davitz, J.R. (1964), *The Communication of Emotional Meaning*. New York, McGraw-Hill.
Davitz, J.R., and Lois, J. (1959), 'Correlates of accuracy in the communication of feelings', *Journal of Communication* 9:110–17.
De Cecco, John P. (1967), *The Psychology of Language, Thought and Instruction*. New York, Holt, Rinehart & Winston.
Derwing, B. L. (1973), *Transformational Grammar as a Theory of Language Acquisition*. Cambridge, Cambridge University Press.
Doke, C. M. (1954), *The Southern Bantu Languages* (Handbook of African Languages). Oxford, Oxford University Press for International African Institute.
Douglas, Jack D. (ed.) (1970), *Deviance and Respectability: The Social Construction of Moral Meanings*. New York, Basic Books.
– (ed.) (1971), *Understanding Everyday Life*. London, Routledge & Kegan Paul.
Dreitzel, P. (ed.) (1971), *Recent Sociology, 2* (Patterns of Communication Behaviour). London, Collier-Macmillan.
Drury, M. O'C. (1973), *The Danger of Words*. London, Routledge & Kegan Paul.
Dunstan, Elizabeth (1969), *Twelve Nigerian Languages*. London, Longmans, Green & Co.

Durbin, Marshall (1966), 'The goals of ethnoscience', *Anthropological Linguistics* 8(8).

Entwistle, Doris R. (1968), 'Developmental sociolinguistics: Inner City Children', *American Journal of Sociology* 74(1): 37–49.

Ferguson, C. A. (1971), *Language Structure and Language Use*. Stanford, Calif., Stanford University Press.

Fillmore, C. J. (1968), 'The case for case', in: *Universals in Linguistic Theory*, ed. by E. Bach and R. T. Harms.

Firth, R. W. (1973), *Symbols Public and Private*. London, George Allen & Unwin.

Fishman, J.A. (ed.) (1968), *Readings in the Sociology of Language*. The Hague, Mouton.

– (1971), *Sociolinguistics: A Brief Introduction*. Rowley, Newbury House.

– (1972), *Advances in the Sociology of Language*, Vol 2. The Hague, Mouton.

Fishman, J. A., et al. (1966), *Language Loyalty in the United States*. The Hague, Mouton.

– (1968), *Language Problems of Developing Nations*. New York, Wiley.

Fodor, J.A., and Katz, J. J. (1964), *The Structure of Language*. Englewood Cliffs, N.J., Prentice-Hall.

Frake, C. O. (1964), 'How to ask for a drink in Subanum', *American Anthropologist* 66(6), Part 2.

Freberg, Stan (n.d.), 'Comedy Caravan' (Gramophone record). Capitol Records T732.

Garfinkel, H. (1967), *Studies in Ethnomethodology*. Englewood Cliffs, N.J., Prentice-Hall.

Gay, J., and Cole, M. (1967), *The New Mathematics and Old Culture*. New York, Holt, Rinehart & Winston.

Ghosh, S. K. (ed.) (1962), *Man, Language and Society*. The Hague, Mouton.

Gigeioli, P. P. (ed.) (1972), *Language and Social Context*. Harmondsworth, Penguin.

Gleason, H.A. (1965), *Linguistics and English Grammar*. New York, Holt, Rinehart & Winston.

Goffman, Erving (1956), 'The nature of deference and demeanour', *American Anthropologist* 58:473–02.

– (1967), *Interaction Ritual*. Garden City, N.Y., Doubleday.

Grayshon, M. C. (1973), 'On saying "No" ', *Nottingham Linguistic Circular* 3(1): 40ff.

– (1975a), 'Some aspects of social grammar features of one type of question in English and Yoruba', *Language in Society*, Spring.

– (1975b), 'Towards a social grammar', *Nottingham Linguistic Circular* 5(1).

Greenberg, J. H. (ed.) (1963), *Universals of Language*. Cambridge, Mass., M.I.T. Press.

– (1968), *Anthropological Linguistics*. New York, Random House.

– (1971), *Language, Culture and Communication*. Stanford, Calif., Stanford University Press.

Greene, Judith (1972), *Psycholinguistics: Chomsky and Psychology*. Harmondsworth, Penguin Education.

Greenfield, Patricia M. (1972), 'Oral or written language: the consequences for the cognitive development in Africa, the United States and England', *Language & Speech* 15, Part 2.

Gumperz, J. J. (1971), *Language in Social Groups*. Stanford, Calif., Stanford University Press.

Gumperz, J. J., and Hymes, D. (eds.) (1964), 'The ethnography of communication', *American Anthropologist* 66(6), Part 2.

– (1972), *Directions in Sociolinguistics*. New York, Holt, Rinehart & Winston.

Hall, E. T. (1959), *The Silent Language*. Garden City, N.Y., Doubleday.

Halliday, M. A. K. (1967), *Intonation and Grammar in British English* (Janua Linguarum Series Practica 48). The Hague, Mouton.

– (1973), *Exploration in the Function of Language*. London, Edward Arnold.

Hartmann, R. R. K., and Stork, F. C. (1973), *Dictionary of Language and Linguistics*. Barking, Applied Science Publishers, Ltd.

Haugen, E. (1971), 'The ecology of language', *The Linguistic Reporter*, Supplement 25, 13(1).

Hayakawa, S. I. (1962), *The Use and Misuse of Language*. Fawcett Publications.

Hertzler, Joyce O. (1965), *A Sociology of Language*. New York, Random House.

Hill, Christopher (1972), *The World Turned Upside Down*. London, Temple Smith.

Hodek, Nada (1967), 'On teaching English intonation to Serbo-Croat learners', *E.L.T.* 22 (1):67.

Hogbin, H. I. (1939), *Experiments in Civilization*. London, Routledge & Kegan Paul.

Hook, Sidney (1960), *Dimensions of Mind*. New York, U. P.

Hsu, Francis L. K. (1969), *The Study of Literate Civilizations*. New York, Holt, Rinehart & Winston.

Huxley, R., and Ingram, E. (eds.) (1968), *Mechanisms of Language Development*. London, Centre for Advanced Study in the Developmental Sciences and C.I.B.A. Foundation.

Hymes, D. (ed.) (1964), *Language in Culture and Society*. New York, Harper & Row.

– (1970), 'Bilingual education: linguistic versus sociolinguistic bases', in: *Bilingualism and Language Contact: Anthropological, Linguistic, Psychological and Sociological Aspects*, ed. by J. Alatis. Monograph Series on Languages and Linguistics, 23. Washington, D. C., Georgetown University Press.

– (1971), *Pidginization and Creolization of Languages*. Cambridge, Cambridge University Press.

Jakobson, R. (1966), *Selected Writings.* The Hague, Mouton.
Jones, S. M. (1959), *Studies in African Music,* Vol. 1. Oxford, Oxford University Press.
Joos, M. (1967), *The Five Clocks.* New York, Harbinger Books.

Keddie, Nell (1973), *Tinker Tailor... The Myth of Cultural Deprivation.* Harmondsworth, Penguin Education.
Kjolseth, R. (1972), 'Making sense', in: *Advances in the Sociology of Language,* vol. 2, ed. by J. A. Fishman. The Hague, Mouton.
Koestler, Arthur (1964), *Acts of Creation.* London, Hutchinson.
Kuhn, Thomas S. (1970), 'The structure of scientific revolutions', *International Encyclopedia of Unified Science,* Vol. 2, No. 2, 2nd ed. Chicago, University of Chicago Press.

Labov, W. (1964), 'Phonological correlates of social stratification', *American Anthropologist* 66(6).
Lamb, Warren (1965), *Posture and Gesture.* Duckworth.
Lapiere, R. T. (1965), *Social Change.* New York, McGraw-Hill.
Laver, J., and Hutcheson, S. (eds.) (1972), *Communication in Face to Face Interaction.* Harmondsworth, Penguin.
Lawton, D. (1968), *Social Class, Language and Education.* London, Routledge & Kegan Paul.
Lenneberg, E. H. (ed.) (1964), *New Directions in the Study of Language.* Cambridge, Mass., M.I.T. Press.
Lieberman, Philip (1967), *Intonation, Perception and Language.* M.I.T. Research Monograph 38. Cambridge, Mass.
– (1973), 'On the evolution of language: a unified view', *Cognition* 2(1).
Lounsbury, F. G. (1956), 'A semantic analysis of Pawnee kinship usage', *Language* 32:158–94.

McIntosh, A., and Halliday, M.A.K. (1966), *Patterns in Language: Papers in General Descriptive and Applied Linguistics.* London, Longmans, Green & Co.
Magee, B. (1973), *Popper.* London, Fontana/Collins.
Meetham, A. R., and Hudson, R. A. (eds.) (1969), *Encyclopedia of Linguistics, Information and Control.* Oxford, Pergamon Press.

Nash, W. (1971), *Our Experience of Language.* Batsford.
Nida, E. A. (1957), *Learning a Foreign Language.* Revised ed. National Council of the Churches of Christ in the U.S.A.
– (1963), *Customs, Culture and Christianity.* Tyndale Press.

Oleson, V., and Whitaker, E. (1968), *The Silent Dialogue.* San Francisco. Jossey Bass.
Open University (1972), *Language in Education: A Source Book.* London, Routledge & Kegan Paul.

Pear, Thomas H. (1955), *English Social Differences*. London, George Allen & Unwin.
- (1957), *Personality, Appearance and Speech*. London, George Allen & Unwin.
Pei, Marco A., and Gaynor, Frank (1954), *A Dictionary of Linguistics*. New York, Philosophical Library.
Pelto, P. J. (1965), *The Study of Anthropology*. Columbus, Ohio, C. E. Merrill Books (Social Science Series).
Pepinsky, Harold B. (ed.) (1970), *People and Information*. New York, Pergamon Press.
Philips, Susan U. (1970), 'Acquisition of rules for appropriate speech usage', in: *Bilingualism and Language Contact: Anthropological, Linguistic, Psychological and Sociological Aspects*, ed. by J. Alatis. Monograph Series on Languages and Linguistics, 23. Washington, D.C., Georgetown University Press.
Piaget, Jean (1959), *The Language and Thought of the Child*. London, Routledge & Kegan Paul.
Pike, K. L. (1946), *Tone Language*. Ann Arbor, Mich., University of Michigan Press.
Polsky, N. (1967), *Hustlers, Beats and Others*. Chicago, Aldine.
Pride, J. B. (1970), *The Social Meaning of Language*. Oxford, Oxford University Press.
Pride, J. B., and Holmes, J. (1972), *Sociolinguistics*. Harmondsworth, Penguin.

Quirk, C.R., Leech, G. N., et al. (1972), *Grammar of Contemporary English*. London, Longmans, Green & Co.

Richards, Jack C. (1972), 'Social factors, interlanguage and language learning', *Language Learning* 22(2):159–88.
Rigby, P. (1968), 'Joking relationships, kin categories and clanship among the Gogo', *Africa* 38(2):133.
Robinson, W. P. (1965a), 'Close procedure as a technique for the investigation of social class differences in language usage', *Language & Speech* 8, Part 1:42.
- (1965b) 'The elaborated code in working class language', *Language & Speech* 8, Part 4: 243.
- (1972), *Language and Social Behaviour*. Harmondsworth, Penguin.
Ross, A. S. C. (1958), *Etymology with Special Reference to English*. London, Deutsch.

Scheflen, A. E. (1972), *Body Language and the Social Order*. Englewood Cliffs, N. J., Prentice-Hall.
Sebeok, T. A., et al. (1966), *Current Trends in Linguistics*, Atlantic Highlands, N.J., Humanities Press.
Sinclair, J. M., et al. (1971), 'School achievement of children with slow speech development'. S. S. R. C. Project Final Report. H. R. 199.
Skinner, B. F. (1957), *Verbal Behaviour*. New York, Appleton-Century Crofts.

Smith, Raymond G. (1970), *Speech Communication: Theory and Models.* New York, Harper & Row.

Spencer, John (1971), *The English Language in West Africa.* London, Longmans, Green & Co.

Steinberg, D. D., and Jacobovits, L. A. (1971), *Semantics: An Interdisciplinary Reader in Philosophy, Linguistics and Psychology.* C.U.P.

Strang, Barbara M. H. (1970), *History of English.* London, Methuen.

Sudnow, D. (1972), *Studies in Social Interactions.* New York, Free Press.

Trager. G. L. (1958), 'Paralanguage: a first approximation', *Studies in Linguistics.* 13(1–2):1–12.

Trager, G. L., and Smith, H. L. (1951), 'Outline of English Structure', *Studies in Linguistics* No. 3. Battenburg, Norman Olda.

Vickers, G. (1955), 'Communication in economic systems', in: *Studies in Communication.* London.

Ward, I. C. (1952). *Introduction to the Yoruba Language.* Cambridge, Heffer.

Watzlawick, P., et al. (1968), *Pragmatics of Human Communication.* London, Faber.

Werner, Heinz (ed.) (n.d.), *On Expressive Language.* Worcester, Mass.

Werner, O. (1966), 'Pragmatics and ethnoscience', *Anthropological Linguistics* 8(8).

West, Michael (1968), *The Minimum Adequate (A Quest).* ELT. 22. 3.

Whitehead, A. N. (1933), *Adventure in Ideas.* Cambridge, Cambridge University Press.

Whitely, W. H. (ed.) (1971), *Language Use and Social Change.* London, Oxford University Press.

Whorf, B. L. (1956), *Language, Thought and Reality,* ed. by J. B. Carroll. Cambridge, Mass., M.I.T. Press.

Williams, Frederick (1970), *Language and Poverty.* Chicago, Markham.

Contributions to the Sociology of Language

Edited by Joshua A. Fishman

1. *Advances in the Sociolgy of Language*
   Volume I: Basic Concepts, Theories and Problems:
   Alternative Approaches
   Ed. by J. A. Fishman
   197, 418 pages, 2nd ed. Clothbound
   ISBN: 90-279-7732-1

2. *Advances in the Sociology of Language*
   Volume II: Selected Studies and Applications
   Ed. by J. A. Fishman
   1972, 534 pages. Paperbound
   ISBN: 90-279-2302-7

3. *Multilingualism in the Soviet Union*
   Aspects of Language Policy and its Implementation
   by E. Glyn Lewis
   1972, xx + 332 pages. Paperbound
   ISBN: 90-279-2352-3

4. *Perspectives on Black English*
   Ed. by J. L. Dillard
   1975, 392 pages. Clothbound
   ISBN: 90-279-7811-5

5. *Advances in Language Planning*
   Ed. by J. A. Fishman
   1974, 590 pages. Paperbound
   ISBN: 90-279-2618-2

6. *The Revival of a Classical Tongue*
Eliezer Ben Yehuda and the Modern Hebrew Language
by Jack Fellman
1973, 152 pages. Paperbound
ISBN: 90-279-2495-3

7. *The Political Sociology of the English Language*
An African Perspective (Who are the Afro-Saxons?)
by Ali A. Mazrui
1975, 232 pages. Clothbound
ISBN: 90-279-7821-2

8. *Advances in the Creation and Revision of Writing Systems*
Ed. by J. A. Fishman
1977, XXVII + 492 pages. Clothbound
ISBN: 90-279-7552-3

9. *Advances in the Study of Societal Multilingualism*
Ed. by J. A. Fishman
1977, approx. 850 pages. Clothbound
ISBN: 90-279-7742-9

10. *Language and Politics*
Ed. by William M. O'Barr and Jean F. O'Barr
1976, XVI + 506 pages. Clothbound
ISBN: 90-279-7761-5

11. *Universalism versus Relativism in Language and Thought*
Proceedings of a Colloquium on the Sapir – Whorf Hypotheses
Ed. by Rik Pinxten
1976, XIV + 310 pages. Clothbound
ISBN: 90-279-7791-7

12. *Selection among Alternatives in Language Standardization*
The Case of Albanian
by Janet Byron
1976, 160 pages. Paperbound
ISBN: 90-279-7542-6

13. *Black Names*
    by J. L. Dillard
    1976, 114 pages. Paperbound.
    ISBN: 90-279-6702-3

14. *Language Planning for Modernization*
    The Case of Indonesian and Malaysian
    by S. Takdir Alisjabana
    1976, 132 pages. Paperbound
    ISBN: 90-279-7712-7

15. *Issues in Sociolinguistics*
    Ed. by Oscar Uribe-Villegas
    1977, 266 pages. Clothbound
    ISBN: 90-279-7722-4

16. *Soviet Contributions to the Sociology of Language*
    Ed. by Philip A. Luelsdorff
    1977, 196 pages. Clothbound
    ISBN: 90-279-7613-9

17. *Acceptability in Language*
    Ed. by Sidney Greenbaum
    1977, X + 214 pages. Clothbound
    ISBN: 90-279-7623-6

18. *Towards a Social Grammar of Language*
    by Matthew C. Grayshon
    1977, 142 pages. Paperbound
    ISBN: 90-279-7633-3

Other volumes are in preparation

MOUTON · THE HAGUE · PARIS